Colaghty Church of Ireland and Tirwinny Methodist Cemeteries, Drumkeeren Parish, County Fermanagh

by

David R. Elliott

Irish Genealogy Series

KinFolk Finders

© David R. Elliott, 2025

This book is not to be copied or put into electronic format without the expressed written permission of Kinfolk Finders.

David R. Elliott, Ph.D., M.Div., is a past-chair of the London & Middlesex Branch of the Ontario Genealogical Society and the founding vice-chair of the organization's Ireland Special Interest Group.

ISBN: 978-1-927357-75-0

Cover photo: Colaghty Parish Church with Section C of its cemetery to the left. (DRE 2019).

KinFolk Finders

154 Main Street, Parkhill

Ontario, Canada N0M 2K0

1-519-294-0728

Preface to the Irish Genealogy Series' New Format

When we first visited Ireland in 2004, we were searching for our Irish ancestors. We soon discovered that so many of its cemeteries had never been indexed. Those that had been done, were done poorly with only the most legible tombstones being recorded, and often the published indexes listed the stones alphabetically without any indication of their location or *in situ* context. Without detailed site maps, it was very difficult locating those stones. Taking our cue from the past cemetery indexing projects of the Ontario Genealogical Society, we felt that a better job could be done for Irish cemeteries.

The 1922 destruction of almost all of the pre-1901 Irish census records and the burning of most of the Church of Ireland (Anglican) parish registers, marriage bonds and wills in the explosion at the General Registry Office in Dublin during the civil war was a great tragedy. We are forced to use all sources available to us to recreate the past; information gained from cemeteries is thus very important.

Preface

With my background in archaeology, we have taken advantage of aerial photography and noting ground cover changes to detect buried stones, employing surveying techniques to map the cemeteries, using plain flour and water to highlight difficult texts, and creating digital photographic techniques to capture the images of hard-to-read inscriptions.

As a historian, I have sought to provide the most accurate reproduction of the information on the tombstones by checking questionable names, dates and ages against surviving parish registers, and civil registrations of births, marriages and deaths. In our transcriptions, we have provided the correct spellings of misspelled townlands, checking locations against the Tithe Applotments, the Griffith Valuation, and surviving census records. The name of the townland is so very important in Irish genealogical research.

In our research of each graveyard, we have keyed the transcriptions according to sections, rows and tombstone numbers to our maps of the cemeteries and their indexes. We have also recorded the spaces which may contain unmarked graves or unused plots. Every name on the tombstones has been recorded in the alphabetical comprehensive index at the back of each book.

Preface

For the Transcriptions of Tombstones section, we have employed various terms to describe the different types of grave markers. We have used the word plot to describe a defined burial area with four borders or different types of fences. Some have perimeter inscriptions on the curbs.

Some types of plots have only one border extending across their width and supports the headstone. We have called these partial plots.

There are various kinds of burial memorials found in the cemeteries. There are free-standing headstones, pedestal markers, temporary wooden crosses with plaques, flat stones, raised flats and sarcophagi (stone coffins above ground), also mausoleums and massive monuments. To help readers identify what we are describing, we have included a selection of different tombstone styles that we have encountered across Ireland.

Our own research and research for our clients has led us to index cemeteries in counties Antrim, Donegal, Fermanagh, Leitrim, Tyrone and also Wicklow. Initially our company, KinFolk Finders, published our indexes in-house, but we are now publishing them in a new format produced by Lightning Source in order to facilitate wider international exposure and ease of access. Eventually, all of our previous titles will be put into this new format. Some

Preface

smaller cemetery indexes will be consolidated with others in the same parish or pastoral charge.

For those who cannot personally visit these Irish cemeteries, we have put our photographs of each tombstone on FindmyPast.ie .

Table of Contents

Preface to Irish Genealogy Series Format.................iii

Table of Contents..1

Introduction..3

Acknowledgements...7

Map of Counties of Ireland................................9

Map of Parishes of County Fermanagh...................10

Map of the Cemetery Locations 11

Maps of the Cemeteries...................................12

Views of the Churches and Cemeteries.................. 13

Bibliography..17

Styles of Tombstones.......................................18

Transcriptions of Colaghty Tombstones..................33

Transcriptions of Tirwinny Methodist Tombstones.......78

Key to Index of Names....................................88

Combined Index 89

List of Irish Genealogy Series Publications..............109

Contents

Introduction

Colaghty or Lack Church of Ireland (Anglican) is located in the north-east portion of County Fermanagh in Northern Ireland. It is near the village of Lack, approximately six miles east of Kesh.

In 1835, church meetings were started in a school house as a Chapel of Ease for the those belonging St. Mary's Ardess Church of Ireland in Magheraculmoney Parish. A church building was built in 1844 on Keeran townland in Drumkeeran Parish. By 1872, it became its own ecclesiastical parish drawing its congregation from townlands transferred from the eastern portion of Magheraculmoney Parish, parts of Drumkeeran Parish, and Longford West Parish of County Tyrone. Burials for its members continued to be done at St. Mary's Ardess until its own cemetery was opened at the Colaghty church in 1874.

We first visited this cemetery in 2019, taking a few photographs, but because of COVID I was not able to get

Introduction

back to properly survey it until late May 2023.

We have recorded every tombstone, consulting death registrations and census data to validate townland names and information. Where the townland names have been misspelled, we have given the correct spelling, followed by an asterisk (*). Townland names have been included in (brackets).

Within the cemetery are large areas that are empty of memorial stones, but most likely those areas contain unmarked graves. In the transcriptions we have marked those areas as spaces, in case memorial headstones or plots are later erected on those spots.

There are some memorials inside the church which we did not have access to, but they have been recorded in David Keys' parish history. Because this index is primarily genealogical, we have not reproduced all of the invocations, supplications, poetry and sayings on the tombstones, as important as they might be to the families who erected them. We have kept those that are necessary for the grammatical sense of the transcriptions.

One problem we have encountered is determining the surnames of people listed on current stones if the second name could be interpreted either as a forename or a last name. For example, plot B2-2 is marked as a Gilmour

Introduction

burial site. The last entry is for a Robert Ferguson. Was Ferguson his second name, or was it the last name of a possible son-in-law or a grandson, the son of a daughter? Because we cannot check the un-released births, marriages and deaths in the civil registrations or the closed parish registers, in this case we have assumed that the second name was actually a second name, unless we knew that it was the married name of his mother.

Some grave stones contain the maiden names of women. At other times, their brothers are listed so the maiden name of the woman can be determined.

We have also included in this book the small Tirwinny Methodist Cemetery which is located on Tirwinny Townland, north-west of Lack, near the intersection of Tirwinny and Tirmacspird Roads. The Methodist Church, which was erected in 1870, is now abandoned with holes in its roof.

The Tirwinny Cemetery contains the graves of people from Fermanagh and Tyrone. We surveyed this cemetery in May of 2019. It is still in use for burials. The graves consist of free standing headstones and family plots. None of the memorial monuments are outstanding in design.

Not only does this cemetery contain the remains of

Introduction

Methodists, but there are also some burials of other sect members such as the Cooneyites (or Evangelists). There is also a reference to a family with some members buried at the Colaghty Church of Ireland.

All of the stones have been photographed and they can be found on *FindmyPast.ie* or ordered directly from Kinfolk Finders.

In searching for earlier information on family members, one should check the St. Mary's Church of Ireland parish registers, the parent church for the Colaghty congregation. We have indexed that church's parish registers from 1763-1918.

Acknowledgements

We are grateful for the assistance given to us by local historian David Keys of Glenarn townland. He kindly gave me a copy of his history of the Colaghty Parish, showed me around the parish hall, and invited me to his home where we discussed his current research on military and policing history of County Fermanagh. He has also promptly answered my email queries pertaining to some inscriptions on the tombstones.

David and Val Bailey of Blaney Caravan Park, have continued to be our gracious hosts and encouragers of our genealogical endeavors in Fermanagh.

Brian Mitchell of Derry kindly allowed us to copy and modify some of his parish maps found in his *A New Genealogical Atlas of Ireland*, 2nd edition. (Baltimore: Genealogical Publishing Co., Inc., 2002).

Nancy Elliott helped survey the Tirwinney Cemetery and prepared the maps displayed in this book.

Acknowledgements

As usual, Linda Smith, while doing copy editing of the text, caught many of my typos and stylistic errors.

Blaney Caravan Park, our home away from home while in Ireland. (DRE 2023).

Counties of Ireland

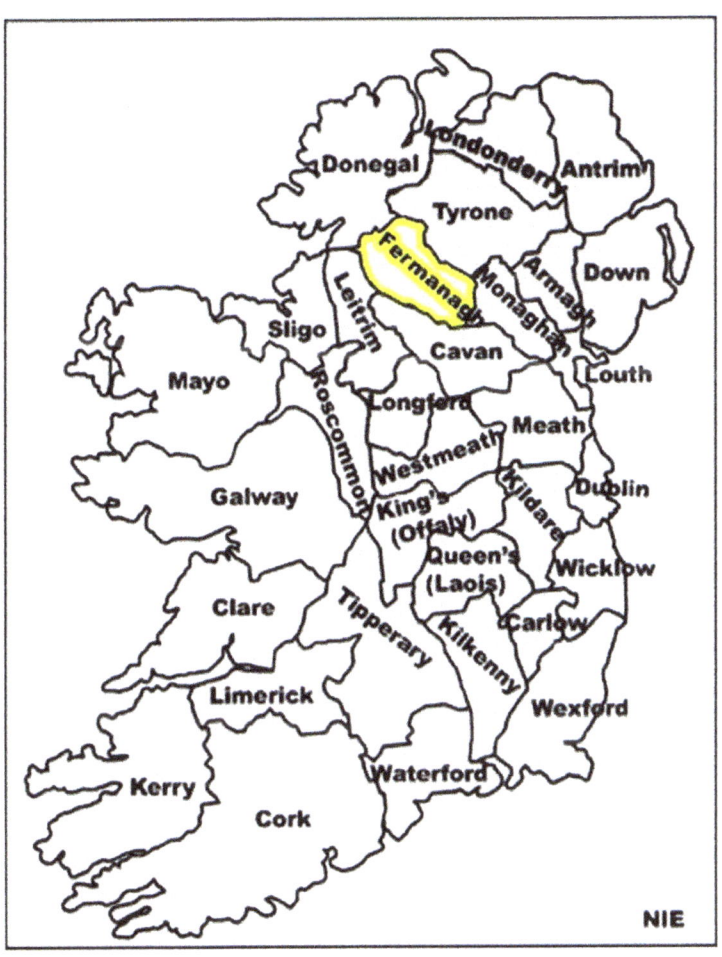

The six counties of Northern Ireland have a darker shading. Fermanagh is the most westerly of them. (NIE 2012).

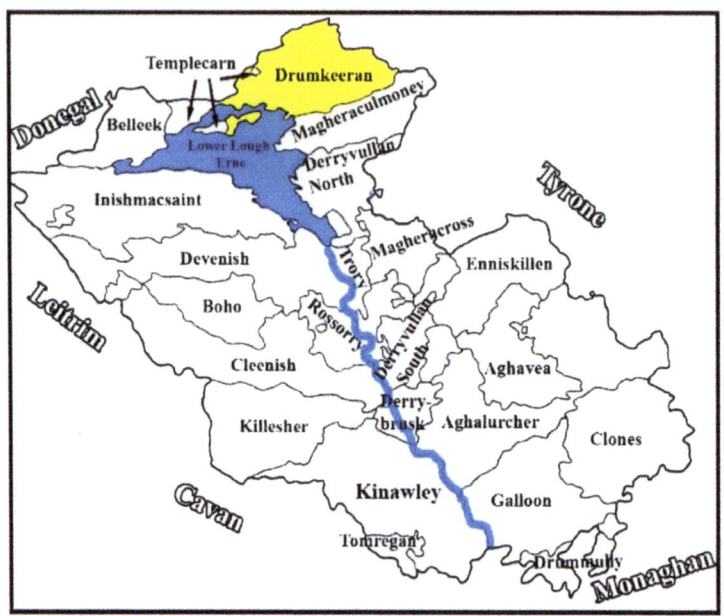

County Fermanagh parishes and the surrounding counties. (NIE 2024).

    This is an approximate map of the parishes of County Fermanagh. It is very difficult to delineate the Upper Lough Erne on a map of this size because it is not a continuous large body of water, but a waterway interspersed with many islands. It is part of the Shannon River system that extends though the interior of Ireland. However, the Upper Lough Erne system becomes wider in places towards the southern border of the county. Drumkeeran Parish, featured in this book, is highlighted in yellow.

Maps

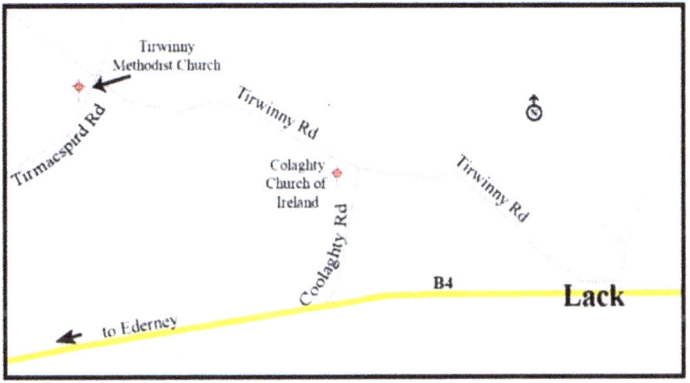

Locations of these cemeteries in Drumkeeren Parish. (NIE 2020).

Cemetery Maps

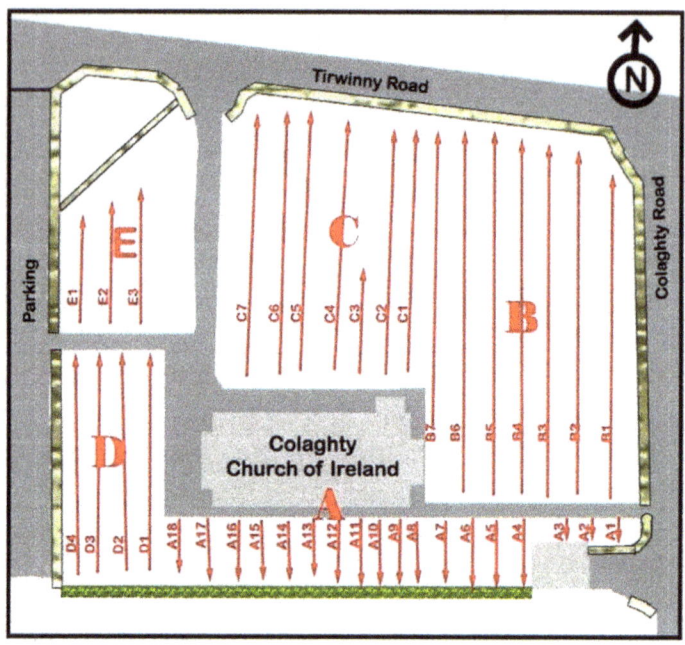

(NIE maps: Colaghty 2024 and Tirwinny 2025).

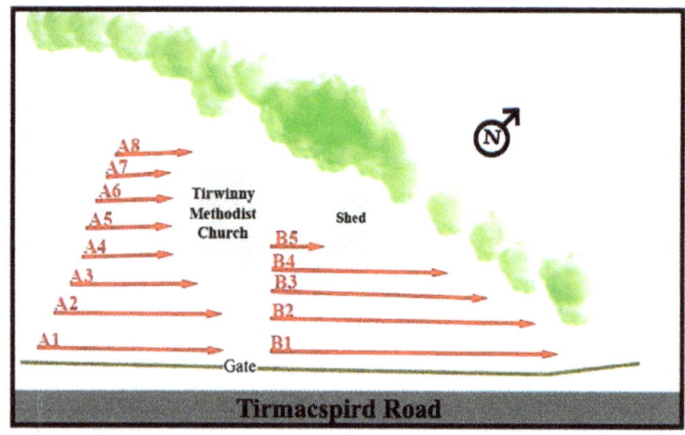

Views of the Cemetery Sections

Section A on south side of church. The ornate headstone is A8-2. (DRE 2019).

Section B on east side of church. (DRE 2023).

Section C on north side of church with many unmarked burials. (DRE 2023).

Cemetery Views

Section D on west side of church. (DRE 2023).

Newly opened Section E to the immediate right with Parish Hall behind. (DRE 2019).

Cemetery Views

Section A. Tirwinny Methodist Cemetery. (DRE 2019).

Section B. (DRE 2019).

Bibliography

Day, Angélique and Patrick McWilliams, eds. *Ordnance Survey Memoirs of Ireland Volume 14: Parishes of Co. Fermanagh II, 1834-5.* Belfast: Institute of Irish Studies, Queen's University, 1992.

Elliott, David R. *A Comprehensive Index of the St. Mary's Ardess Church of Ireland, Magheraculmoney Parish Registers, County Fermanagh, 1763-1918.* Parkhill: Kinfolk Finders, 2021.

Keys, David. *Lack or Colaghty Parish 1835-2002.* Belleek: Erne Heritage Tour Guides, 2002.

Leslie, J.B. et al. *Clergy of Clogher.* Belfast: Ulster Historical Foundation, 2006.

Mitchell, Brian. *A New Genealogical Atlas of Ireland*, 2nd edition. (Baltimore: Genealogical Publishing Co., Inc., 2002).

Styles of Tombstones

Plots

Plot: a burial area with four defined borders. (Fivemiletown, DRE 2024).

A fenced plot with a pillar headstone with inscriptions on all four sides. (Monea, DRE 2006).

Fenced plot with large funeral monument having architectural features. (Old Aghalurcher, DRE 2024).

Caged plot. (Monea, DRE 2023).

Partial plots with only one border, extending the full width of the burial area. (Colaghty, DRE 2023).

Flats

A large flat flagstone memorial. (Old Aghalurcher, DRE 2024).

Crested flat stone with heraldic crest above memorial text. (Old Aghalurcher, DRE 2024).

Raised flat or table monument with an inscription. (Garrison, DRE 2008).

Types of Headstones

Simple free-standing headstone. Older ones often have sunk into the ground, burying the lower rows of the inscriptions. (Monea, DRE 2006).

Tombstone Styles

Military marker erected by the Commonwealth War Graves Commission. (Benmore, DRE 2007).

Small iron Celtic crosses. (Derrygonnelly, (DRE 2009).

Tombstone Styles

Fancy children's burial markers. (Fivemiletown, DRE 2011).

Children's plot with toys. (Fivemiletown, DRE 2024).

High Celtic cross in a plot. (Ederney, DRE 2023).

Stubby Celtic cross headstone. (Edenclaw, DRE 2023).

Roman cross headstone. (Edenclaw, DRE 2023).

Pedestal marker. (Garrison, DRE 2009).

Temporary wooden cross with plaque. (Belcoo, DRE 2015).

Inscription on perimeter border of plot. (Derrbybrusk, DRE 2016).

Book-shaped marker. (Derrygonnelly, DRE 2009).

Tombstone Styles

Inscribed flower holder; sometimes containing genealogical data. (Tubrid, DRE 2016).

Scroll-shaped headstones. (Derrybrusk, DRE 2016).

Sarcophagii

A sarcophagus is an above-ground stone coffin. (Benmore, DRE 2007).

Fancy low-profile sarcophagus. (Ballyshannon, DRE 2015).

Mausoleums

Mausoleums can be large above-ground burial structures or large underground rooms for the burials of wealthy families as below. (Aghavea, DRE 2012).

Mausoleum. (Ardess, DRE 2019).

Colaghty Church of Ireland Cemetery

Transcriptions of Colaghty Tombstones

Section A

A1-1 [**BUCHANAN** plot]. In loving memory of **Robert Buchanan**, died 17th August 1973, aged 91 years. Also his loving wife **Mary Wilson** died 20th February 1986, aged 95 years.

A2-1 [Plot with iron railings; headstone has missing lead letters]. In loving memory of **John Patton** (Tirwinny*) who died Oct. 12th 1900, aged 75 years. Also his son **Robert Patton** who died July 7th 1900, aged 33 years. His daughter **Mary Anne Patton** who died May 28th 1902, aged 39 years. Also his wife **Eleanor Patton** who died July 22nd 1920, aged 95 years. [Civil registration has her age as 97].

A3-1 [**MILLIGAN** plot; no names listed].

Colaghty Church of Ireland Cemetery

ROW A4

A4-1 [Headstone with lead letters missing; masonic crest at top.] Erected by **Wm. H. Acheson** of Meenaheery [Tyrone] to the memory of his dearly beloved son **William Henry Acheson**, N.S.T. [National School Teacher], who departed this life on the 21st April 1897, aged 38 years.

A4-2 [spaces].

ROW A5

A5-1 [Plot]. In loving memory of **Robert Wilson** (Stranahone), died 21st Aug. 1941, aged 84 years. And his wife **Mary** died 28th July 1944, aged 86 years. Also his brother **John** died 25th September 1941, aged 82 years. The undermentioned **Robert** died 16 Dec. 1973, aged 76 years. **Henrietta Wilson**, J.P., wife of **Robert**, died 4th April 1978, aged 74 years. Erected by their son **Robert**.

A5-2 [**JOHNSTON** plot]. In loving memory of **Joseph Johnston** (Stranadarriff*), died 22nd July 1967, aged 72 years. Also grandchildren: **Norah** died 16th July 1969, aged 13 months. **Gary** died 8th August 1975, aged 8 years. And wife **Isabella** died 19th December 1988, aged 92 years.

A5-3 [**LITTLE** plot]. In loving memory of **Henry (Harry)**, died 29th June 1958. His wife **Sarah** died 29th

Colaghty Church of Ireland Cemetery

July 1985. His son **Henry (Harry)** died 30th April 1985. Also infant daughters.

ROW A6

A6-1 **[ACHESON** plot]. In loving memory of **Evelyn**, died 29th April 1944, aged 24 years. **George** died 22nd May 1947, aged 86 years. **Margaret** died 17th January 1952, aged 93 years. **William** died 21st July 1984, aged 84 years.

A6-2 [space].

A6-3 **[JOHNSTON** partial plot]. In loving memory of **James (Jim) Johnston**, died 27th December 1965, aged 82 years. His brother **Robert (Bob)** died 1st May 1966, aged 76 years. Their cousin **Minnie Gilmour** died 12th December 1961, aged 80 years. And their niece **Elizabeth Johnston** died 29th August 2011, aged 98 years.

ROW A7

A7-1 [space].

A7-2 [Headstone]. Erected in loving remembrance of **Anne Jane**, wife of **Caldwell Barton** who died 1st Sept. 1884, aged 50 years. [Plaque]. In memory of **William John Barton** 1900-1945, loved husband of **Dinah**, father of Ida, Bill, Noll, Martha, George, Daisy and Mervyn.

A7-3 [BARTON headstone]. In loving memory of **Andrew Barton**, died 28th Nov. 1981. Also his wife **Ann** died 22nd Jan. 2007.

A7-4 [**WEIR** plot with iron railings]. In loving memory of **John Weir** (Meilroe [Oghillicartan*]) died 21st June 1920. His wife **Annie** died 5th December 1947. Their son **William** died 24th February 1985. Their daughters: **Rose** died 3rd July 1952. And **Margaret Jane** died 6th July 1973.

A7-5 [narrow space].

ROW A8

A8-1 [Plot with iron railings; some lead letters on headstone missing]. In loving memory of **Mary Jane Davis** who departed this life on the 14th day of August 1892, aged 47 years. [At bottom]. Erected by her husband and family.

A8-2 [Plot with iron railings; fancy headstone]. Sacred to the memory of **William John Johnston** (Tirmacspird*), died 30th July 1893, aged 71 years. Also his son **William Johnston** died 1st June 1875, aged 20 years. And **Kathleen Johnston**, the beloved wife of **Charles Johnston** of Bracklin, died 11th March 1895, aged 35 years. Also **Margaret Johnston**, wife of **William John**

Colaghty Church of Ireland Cemetery

Johnston, died July 2nd 1910, aged 82 years. **Robert John** died 4th March 1985, aged 84 years. Also his wife **Violet Maud** died 26th June 2003, aged 87 years. And their son **Kenneth** died 4th March 2011, aged 61 years.

A8-3 [Plot with headstone; lead lettering]. In loving memory of **William John Kerr** (Edenaclogh*) who died 27th Feb. 1896, aged 60 years. And his son **Joseph Kerr** who died 27th Nov. 1892, aged 10 years. Also his wife **Margaret Kerr** who died 5th May 1896, aged 50 years. Erected by **John Kerr**.

ROW A9

A9-1 [**KEYS** plot]. (Dullaghan, [Tyrone]). In loving memory of a devoted wife, mother and grandmother **Margaret Isobel**, died 30th December 1998, aged 75 years. Also a devoted husband, father and grandfather **George Victor** died 22nd July 2001, aged 78 years.

A9-2 [**CROZIER** plot]. In loving memory of **Margaret Crozier**, died 1st March 1915, aged 55 years. And her husband **Francis** died 20th June 1934, aged 85 years. Also their daughter **Annie Jane** died 20th December 1963, aged 76 years. Also their son **Charles** died 10th Oct. 1966, aged 82 years. Erected by **Charles Crozier** of Drumbrick.

A9-3 [Plot with headstone with lead letters; a second inscription in a different font is hardly legible. Its text in

Colaghty Church of Ireland Cemetery

italics has been supplied by David Keys]. Erected by **John Vance** (Oghill) in memory of his beloved wife **Mary** who died Feb. 24th 1892, aged 60 years. Also his daughter **Mary Anne** died 26th 1893, aged 24 years. *Also* **William John Caldwell** *died April 7th 1939, aged 75 years. And his wife* **Elizabeth Caldwell** *died April 4th 1959, aged 81 years.*

ROW A10

A10-1 [space].

A10-2 [**KEYS** headstone]. In loving memory of **Rebecca Florence** (*nee* **Buchanan**) who departed this life 12th December 2003, aged 86 years. **Anna Elizabeth Cuzner** (*nee* **Keys**) died 12th August 2010, aged 86 years. **Samuel (Sam)** died 11th May 2013, aged 87 years.

A10-3 [White headstone]. Erected by **Samuel Keys** in memory of his father **Irvine Keys**, died 1st June 1898, aged 87 years. Also his mother **Jane** died 16th July 1903, aged 93 years. Also his wife **Eliza Jane** died 16th April 1924, aged 74 years. **Samuel Keys** died 20th March 1926, aged 74 years. Also his daughter-in-law **Lizzie Jane**, wife of **Samuel Keys Jr.**, died 9th June 1947, aged 50 years. And his daughter **Elizabeth** died 11th October 1957, aged 73 years. Also his son **Robert John Keys**, husband of **Minnie Keys**, died 20th December 1959, aged 77 years.

Colaghty Church of Ireland Cemetery

Samuel Keys, husband of the above Lizzie Jane, died 12th May 1974, aged 86 years. (Glenarn).

A10-4 [space].

ROW A11

A11-1 [Plot]. In loving memory of Laurence Whitcombe (Noble Hall), died 8th November 1970. His wife Eileen Mary died 10th November 1976.

A11-2 [KEYS plot]. In loving memory of Isabella, died 4th January 1938, aged 62 years. Charles died 5th October 1938, aged 65 years. And their son William John died 1st February 1967, aged 57 years. His wife Annabel died 22nd September 1996, aged 76 years.

A11-3 [Lid of a large sarcophagus propped up against its structure which has filled in and grassed over]. Erected by Charles Keys (Glenarn) in memory of his mother Anne Keys who departed this life March 16th 1874, aged 70 yrs. Also his father Charles Keys who departed this life April 1st 1879, aged 77 yrs. [Civil registration has her age as 74 and his as 76.]

ROW A12

A12-1 [space].

A12-2 [unmarked grave with five flower domes].

A12-3 [spaces].

ROW A13

A13-1 [**BRATTON** plot]. In loving memory of **George Bratton**, died 13th October 1973, aged 71 years. And his wife **Margaret Maria** died 24th August 1979, aged 74 years. Also their daughter **Florence Kathleen Moore** died 4th June 2017, aged 74 years.

A13-2 [spaces].

ROW A14

A14-1 [**ROBINSON** plot]. In loving memory of **Hugh**, died 2nd Oct. 1973, aged 91 years. His wife **Mary** died 20th July 1932, aged 52 years. Interred in Irvinestown* Churchyard. Also their son **James** died 30th November 1999, aged 79 years.

A14-2 [**OLDMAN** plot with headstone and perimeter inscriptions]. In loving memory of **George** who died 14th November 1985, aged 74 years. His son **Thomas James** murdered by the I.R.A. on 3rd April 1987, aged 39 years.

His wife **Mary** who died 2nd February 2003, aged 79 years. Also their son **William George** who died 5th March 2016, aged 65 years. [Perimeter]. **Arthur Patton** died 12th October 1945. And wife **Margaret** died 2nd November 1958.

ROW A15

A15-1 [White granite **McBRYDE** plot; difficult to read]. In loving memory of **Ethel Elizabeth**, died 28th May 1987.

A15-2 [**WILSON** plot]. In loving memory of **Olie Wilson**, died 4th November 1981, aged 88 years. And his wife **Margaret Ann** died 23rd July 1983, aged 88 years.

A15-3 [unmarked grave with four flower domes].

A15-4 [space].

ROW A16

A16-1 [**ARMSTRONG** plot]. In loving memory of **Thomas Armstrong** (Stranahone), died 21st March 1992, aged 96 years. And his wife **Margaret Jane** died 4th April 1988, aged 81 years.

A16-2 [Plot with decorative iron railings; lead letters on headstone; difficult to read]. Erected by **William Barton** of Drumgowna in loving memory of his daughter **Maggie** who departed this life 28th Sept. 1893, aged 43 years. [Civil registration has her age as 42].

A16-3 [spaces with mound].

ROW A17

A17-1 [**NELSON** plot]. In loving memory of **Annabella Nelson** (Kilsmullan*), died 16th July 1975, aged 68 years. And her husband **Alfred** died 1st June 1982, aged 78 years.

A17-2 [Plot]. To the memory of the **Speer** Family (Largy).

ROW A18

A18-1 [**BEACOM** plot]. Everlasting memories of a dear wife and mother **Violet Maud** (Drumboarty*), died 24th May 1985, aged 66 yrs. And also husband **Albert** died 20th May 1990, aged 73 yrs.

A18-2 [**BRATTON** plot]. In loving memory of **William**, died 12th March 1947, aged 90 yrs. His wife **Elizabeth** died 4th Nov. 1941, aged 75 yrs. **Samuel Thomas** died 10th Aug. 1953, aged 62 yrs. His wife **Sarah Jane** died 10th Oct. 1961, aged 71 yrs. **Robert** died 21st Sept. 1965, aged 70 yrs.

Colaghty Church of Ireland Cemetery

A18-3 [space].

SECTION B

ROW B-1

B1-1 [**WEIR** plot]. In loving memory of a dear son and brother **Noel**, died 16th April 1995, aged 25 years. Also his grandparents: **Mary Jane** died 23rd August 1968, aged 73 years. **James** died 30th March 1972, aged 89 years. And his father **David Alfred** died 29th November 1995, aged 76 years. And his mother **Martha Isobel Jean** died 13th October 2004, aged 75 years.

B1-2 [**JOHNSTON** plot]. (Lack). In loving memory of **William Johnston**, died 12th Feb. 1947, aged 73 years. Also his wife **Sarah Jane** died 18th Oct. 1969, aged 78 years. Also their son **Robert James** died 2nd Aug. 1985, aged 71 years. His wife **Annie Eileen** died 25th March 2021, aged 92 years.

B1-3 [Plot]. In loving memory of **John Crozier** (Drumcose), died 22nd Sept. 1942, aged 85. Also his wife **Elizabeth** died 11th Feb. 1956, aged 80. And their infant daughter **Elizabeth** died 5th March 1902, aged 1 year. And their son **William** died 14th June 1966, aged 54. Their daughter **Georgina Mabel** died 23rd July 1985, aged 72. And their son **John** died 5th October 1985, aged 80.

B1-4 [**FOSTER** plot with four perimeter inscriptions]. In loving and precious memories of a devoted wife and mother **Elizabeth Mary** (*nee* **Johnston**), born 1916, died 31st March 2001. Her husband **George Hamilton [Foster]** died 26th October 2005, aged 86 years. Their loving son **Percy** died 4th October 2020, aged 66 years. Dear son **Victor** died 1945, aged 5 months. [Perimeter inscriptions]. **Robert Victor Foster** died 10th Dec. 1945, aged 5 mths. **Percy Foster**, loving husband of **Kim**, a dear brother, father and grandfather. **Elizabeth Johnston** died 14th July 1940, aged 58 years. **W.J. Johnston** died 28th July 1955, aged 76 years.

B1-5 [spaces].

B1-6 [**VIRTUE** plot with two perimeter inscriptions]. In loving memory of **Mary Ann**, the beloved wife of **Thomas Virtue** of Glenarn, who died 16th April 1929, aged 66 years. Also her husband **Thomas** died 29th March 1951, aged 88 years. And their son **Joseph** died 13th March 1975, aged 78 years. Also his wife **Isobella** died 25th February 1958, aged 54 years. And their infant son **Noel** died 30th August 1942, aged 8 months. [Perimeter inscriptions]. **Johnston Virtue** 1871-1950. Also his wife **Margaret Ann** 1884-1949. And infant daughter **Violet Susan** died 1911, aged 7 weeks. **George Virtue** 1869-1948. Also his wife **Elizabeth** 1882-1947. And great granddaughter Baby **Elizabeth** died 23rd January 1957.

Colaghty Church of Ireland Cemetery

B1-7 [**BROWN** headstone]. In loving memory of **Mary** (*nee* **Adams**), died 17th March 1967, aged 67 years. And her loving husband **Jacob** died 12th August 1971, aged 83 years. Also their daughter **Harriett May** died 4th August 2011, aged 85 years.

B1-8 [spaces and mounds].

B1-9 [**LIVINGSTONE** headstone]. In loving memory of our dear parents: **Violet Margaret** (*nee* **Brown**), died 31st July 1971, aged 42 years. **Norman David** died 20th Oct. 1983, aged 60 years.

B1-10 [**KILFEDDER** plot]. In loving memory of **Elizabeth**, died 16th Dec. 1987, aged 68 years. Also **Annie Goddard** died 22nd Sept. 1981, aged 80 years. And **Robert**, husband of **Elizabeth**, died 28 Sept. 1991, aged 81 years.

B1-11 [spaces to the end of the row].

ROW B2

B2-1 [space].

B2-2 [**GILMOUR** plot]. In loving memory of **William James Gilmour**, died 4th August 1973, aged 62 years. **James** died 12th December 1974, aged 96 years. **Sarah Jane** died 20th August 1958, aged 82 years. **Ivy Gladys** died 30th March 1983, aged 62 years. **Robert Ferguson** died 11th December 1993, aged 77 years.

B2-3 [spaces].

B2-4 [**EMERY** plot with two **REEVES** plaques]. In loving memory of **Sarah**, died 19th April 1917, aged 75 years. Also her husband **Alexander** died 20th January 1924, aged 84 years. Their daughters: **Elizabeth** died 11th September 1940, aged 55 years. **Matilda** died 8th December 1947, aged 64 years. [Plaque 1]. **REEVES**. In loving memory of **Clive Desmond Alexander**, died 30th May 2006, aged 90 years. And his dear wife **Patricia Elizabeth** died 29th Nov. 2003, aged 88 years. [Plaque 2]. **Sarah Ann Reeves** (*nee* **Emery**) died London, 18th January 1937, aged 50 years. Loved mother of **Clive**, **Betty Tubman** (Ashburton, New Zealand), and **Jim** (Crumlin).

B2-5 [space with mounds].

B2-6 [Plot]. In loving memory of **Thomas Johnston** (Knockroe), died 25th Sept. 1928, aged 74 years. Also his wife **Annie Elizabeth** died 15th Feb. 1938, aged 72 years. And their son **Chadwalder Blaney Johnston** died 31st Dec. 1974, aged 81 years. Also **Margaret Jane Johnston**, beloved wife of **Samuel S. Johnston** of Queensland, Australia, died 13th August 1972, aged 53 years.

B2-7 [**IRVINE** plot]. In fondest memory of **Ethel Mary Ruth Irvine**, L.D.S., R.C.S.I., dearly loved wife of **Robert H. Irvine** (Strabane), who died 9th May 1966. Also the above **Robert H. Irvine** who died 18th August 1979. Sadly missed by his second wife **Ida**. **Ida Irvine** who died 7th September 1982.

B2-8 [Grey granite **BEACOM** plot with three perimeter inscriptions]. **Joseph Beacom** died 23rd July 1986. **Elizabeth Jane Beacom** died 20th Nov. 1973. **William James Kirkpatrick** died 31st May 1961, aged 10 weeks.

B2-9 [spaces].

B2-10 [Plot]. In loving memory of **James Smith**, died 25th Nov. 1965, aged 93 years. Veteran of the Boer and 1914-1918 Wars.

B2-11 [**IRVINE** plot]. In loving memory of **Margaret Irvine**, died 21st Dec. 1967, aged 76 years. And her husband **John James** died 5th Aug. 1969, aged 71 years. Their son **Robert Henry (Bobby)** died 19th June 2000, aged 71 years.

B2-12 [spaces to the end of row].

ROW B3

B3-1 [Large **NOBLE** plot with four perimeter inscriptions. David Keys has identified the surnames of **Fred** and **Brian** below.] In loving memory of the **Noble** Family (Oghill). **Magovern, Isabel** died 8th Jan. 1919. [Civil registration had her death on 7th Jan. 1920. Her marriage record indicates her father was **John Noble**.] **Fred [Curtis]** died 18th July 1984. **Curtis, Anne** died 20th April 1992. **Brian [Curtis]** died 23rd July 1960. [There is an old large flagstone leaning up against the railings of a large plot in B4 that belonged to B3-1 before it was modernized.] Erected by **John Noble** (Oghill) in memory of his father **John Noble** who departed this life 8th March 1878, aged 76 yrs.

B3-2 [**WEIR** plot]. In loving memory of **Thomas John**, died 28th January 1947. His wife **Selina Mary** died 20th June 1965. Their grandson **William Herbert** died 6th April 1983. Their son **Nelson** died 27th February 1992, aged 78 years. And his wife **Edith Mary** died 30th October 1993, aged 77 years.

B3-3 [**WOODS** plot]. In loving memory of our dear parents: **Thomas** died 4th September 1957. **Annie** died 12th November 1979. Their grandson **Kenneth Russell** died 25th August 1984. His father **Thomas** died 29th November 2001. Also **Isabella Jane**, wife of **Thomas**, died 13th December 2022.

B3-4 [**KILFEDDER** plot; white headstone with gold lettering]. In loving memory of our dear father & mother. **John Kilfedder** died 17th Feb. 1946. **Annie Kilfedder**

Colaghty Church of Ireland Cemetery

died 6th Sept. 1951. **Samuel** 1914-1974. **Edward J.** 1898-1977. **Florrie**, wife of **Edward**, 1911-2005.

B3-5 [spaces and mounds].

B3-6 [**EVANS** plot]. In loving memory of **George Evans**, died 23rd January 1924, aged 86 years. His wife **Mary Jane** died 18th May 1914, aged 76 years. Their son **George Stewart** died 7th October 1947, aged 72 years. His wife **Elizabeth Catherine** died 29th May 1961, aged 72 years. Their son **George Evans** died 6th July 1998, aged 88 years.

B3-7 [spaces with mounds].

B3-8 [**RANKIN** plot]. In loving memory of **John**, died 1st April 1968, aged 91 years. His wife **Annabella** died 21st Oct. 1975, aged 73 years. Also their darling little grandson **David Ryan** died 30th March 1981, aged 2 months. Also their son **William** died 7th July 1988, aged 55 years.

B3-9 [**JOHNSTON** plot]. In loving memory of **Robert**, died 29th September 1970. Also his wife **Dorothy (Dora)** died 23rd October 1994.

B3-10 [space].

Colaghty Church of Ireland Cemetery

ROW B4

B4-1 [**WEIR** plot]. In loving memory of our dear mother **Ellen**, died 7th February 1962, aged 77 years. And our dear father **John** died 1st August 1962, aged 86 years.

B4-2 [Huge railed plot that extends into B5. Heavily eroded and or vandalized. Top of sarcophagus has holes and the lead letter inscription destroyed. [David Keys has supplied the missing text.] *In memory of* **Isabella Anne**, *the beloved wife of the Revd.* **E.M. Weir** *and eldest daughter of the late* **John Murray** *of Marfield. Born 22nd November 1837, died 1st Dec. 1876.*

B4-3 [Railed plot; headstone with lead letters missing. Masonic crest]. In loving memory of **Robert Simpson** (Kilsmullan*) who died 24th May 1888, aged 50 years. Also his wife **Mary Anne** who died 6th July 1910, aged 68 years. Their son **William George** who died 14th May 1923, aged 47 years.

B4-4 [space].

B4-5 [Headstone]. In loving memory of the **Wilkin** Family (Croneen Bar*).

B4-6 [space].

B4-7 [Plot]. In loving memory of the **Weir** Family (Knockroe).

B4-8 [space with mounds].

Colaghty Church of Ireland Cemetery

B4-9 [**MARSHALL** plot with decorative iron railing; pink granite headstone]. In loving memory of my father **George Marshall** who died 16th February 1917, aged 98 years. Also my mother **Erwin** who died 5th March 1904, aged 78 years. Also my brother **Thomas** who died 19th April 1903, aged 35 years. Also my uncle **John** who died 28th April 1902, aged 66 years. Erected by **Eva Marshall** (Tirmacspird*).

B4-10 [space with mounds].

B4-11 [Narrow plot]. In loving memory of **Mary Ann Leonard**, died 22 May 1942, aged 82 years. Also **Mary Ann Smith**, wife of the late **James Smith** (Lack), died 28th February 1975, aged 80 years.

B4-12 [spaces].

B4-13 [unmarked grave with two flower domes].

B4-14 [**BROWN** plot]. In loving memory of **Margaret**, died 26th Nov. 1967, aged 65 years. **Edward James** died 8th Feby. 1971, aged 73 years. **Clive** died 18th Sept. 1994, aged 19 years. **Dorothy Rose Elizabeth** died 5th March 1997, aged 89 years.

B4-15 [**SCOTT** plot]. (Glenarn, Lack). In loving memory of **Mary Ann (Minnie)**, died 21st May 1973, aged 63 years.

ROW B5

B5-1 [**KEYS** plot]. In loving memory of **Robert Ernest**, died 24th July 1979, aged 60 years. His mother **Mary Eveline (Minnie)** died 28th April 1984, aged 91 years.

B5-2 [extension of B4-2].

B5-3 [**JOHNSTON** plot; lead letters missing; no details but 1937].

B5-4 [**WOODS** headstone]. In loving memory of a dear father. **Joseph** died 25th September 1974.

B5-5 [space].

B5-6 [Plot with double iron railings]. In memory of **Andrew Barton** who died Nov. 10th 1885, aged 83 years.

B5-7 [unmarked grave with three flower domes].

B5-8 [**HUGHES** plot]. In loving memory of **William John**, died 19th March 1992, aged 69 years. And his son **Norman Addison** died 29th May 2000, aged 45 years. Also a devoted wife and mother **Margaret Isobella (Peggy)** died 28th October 2005, aged 78 years.

B5-9 [spaces and mounds].

B5-10 [**JOHNSTON** plot]. In loving memory of **Thomas Johnston** (Drumcose), died 7th January 1924, aged 47 years. His daughter **Elizabeth** died 7th March 1936, aged 13 years. And his wife **Lily** died 14th June 1962, aged 79

Colaghty Church of Ireland Cemetery

years. Their son **David** died 3rd December 1991, aged 75 years.

B5-11 [space].

B5-12 [unmarked grave with flower dome].

B5-13 [unmarked grave with flower dome].

B5-14 [spaces and mounds].

ROW B6

B6-1 [Plot with large pillar monument dated 15th June 1909]. In affection remembrance of **William Davis**, died 5th July 1876, aged 88 years. Also his wife **Mary Davis** died 12th July 1876, aged 62 years. [Base]. Erected to the memory of the above by their son **Henry Davis**, Eureka, Richmond River, New South Wales.

B6-2 [**HALL** plot]. In loving memory of **William Whitcombe Hall** who died 27th May 1931. **Sarah Mary Hall** who died 2nd January 1943.

B6-3 [space with mound].

B6-4 [**INGRAM** plot]. In loving memory of **James**, died 25th January 1960 and his wife **Mary Jane** died 5th May 1959.

B6-5 [space with mound].

Colaghty Church of Ireland Cemetery

B6-6 [Headstone with lead letters missing]. In loving memory of **Edward Wilson** (Tirwinny*) who died Feby. 3rd 1892, aged 74 years. And also his beloved wife **Sarah** who died Jany. 27th 1897, aged 70 years. Erected by their daughter **Isabella Wilson**.

B6-7 [spaces with mounds].

B6-8 [**DAVIS** plot]. In loving memory of **William Davis** who died 6th April 1941, aged 72 years. Also his wife **Mary** who died 15th Jan. 1938, aged 76 years. And their son **William** who died 23rd Feb. 1907, aged 6 years.

B6-9 [spaces with mounds].

B6-10 [**WOODS** headstone broken off its base]. In loving memory of **Anthony Woods** (Meenmos-sogue*, [Tyrone]), born August 14, 1831, died March 3, 1924.

B6-11 [**KNOX** plot]. In loving memory of our dear parents: **William** died 21st December 1955. **Martha Emily** died 7th February 1987. Also grandparents: **John** died 8th August 1935. **Margaret** died 4th April 1944.

B6-12 [**LITTLE** plot]. In loving memory of **Robert**, died 25 Sept. 1971, aged 93 years. His wife **Elizabeth Mary** died 15th November 1983, aged 73 years. Their son **Edward** died 15th June 1941, aged 3 years. Infant granddaughter **Amanda** died 8th August 1978. Their son **Ivan James** died 8th June 2020, aged 80 years.

Colaghty Church of Ireland Cemetery

B6-13 [Plot with grey granite headstone]. In loving memory of **Joseph Ovens** (Glenarn), died 30th Nov. 1946, aged 83 years.

B6-14 [**LAFFERTY** plot]. In loving memory of **Florence**, died 1st September 1961, aged 1 month. Her brother **Kenneth** died 3rd March 1964, aged 6 months. Also their father **Patrick Joseph** died 16th May 1989, aged 63 years. Also a loving wife and devoted mother **Annabella (Cissie)** died 9th June 2007, aged 76 years. Also their son **William James** died 31st July 2017, aged 57 years.

ROW B7 [last row at east end of church].

B7-1 [spaces to the end of the rear extension of church].

B7-2 [**MILLIGAN** plot]. Treasured memories of **Trevor Thomas James** aged 39 years. Also his wife **Sharron Anne Jayne** aged 30 years. And their unborn baby tragically died together on 5th December 2001.

B7-3 [**McCREA** plot]. In loving memory of **George Ivan**, died 18th December 1996, aged 64 years. Also his son **Rodney Thomas John** died 14th December 2015, aged 46 years.

B7-4 [**SCOTT** plot; text re-arranged because it was awkward]. In loving memory of **Alexander**, died 27th

November 1965. **Mary Lena Todd** (formally [*sic*] **Scott**) died 11th December 2009.

B7-5 [Plot with decorative iron railings; no identification].

B7-6 [Plot]. In memory of the **Farrell** Family (Corlaght). Erected by **Abraham Farrell**.

B7-7 [**GRAHAM** plot]. In loving memory of **John James (Jim)**, died 1st December 1994, aged 84 years. His daughter **Joan Kathleen** died 17th July 2000, aged 50 years. His wife **Jane** (*nee* **Kilfedder**) died 6th December 2001, aged 84 years. **James Kilfedder** died 23rd November 1942, aged 55 years. His wife **Catherine** died 4th October 1968, aged 84 years.

B7-8 [spaces with mounds].

B7-9 [**BEATTIE** plot]. In loving memory of **William Beattie**, died 28th September 1936. His wife **Elizabeth Jane** died 6th April 1952. Also their son-in-law **David Wilson** died 5th October 1982, aged 74 years. Also his wife **Elizabeth Mary** died 22nd November 1993, aged 86 years.

B7-10 [**EVANS** plot]. In loving memory of **Oliver Evans** (Stranahone), died 1st March 1942, aged 46 years. Also his grandson died [in] infancy. His wife **Emily Rebecca** died 7th November 1989, aged 84 years. And their son **William Andrew** died 1st June 1991, aged 63 years.

B7-11 [**WEIR** plot]. In loving memory of **William John**, died 2nd November 1944, aged 71 years. His wife **Martha Jane** died 22nd August 1951, aged 46 years. **Andrew** died 5th March 1945, aged 73 years.

B7-12 [spaces].

SECTION C

ROW C1 (starts with building extension on north side).

C1-1 [**MILLIGAN** plot]. In loving memory of **Thomas Andrew (Tommie)**, died 3rd June 2009, aged 77 years.

C1-2 [**HICKS** plot]. In loving memory of **William James**, died 8th October 1943, aged 51 years. And his son **Robert James** died 13th September 1981, aged 60 years. Also **Elizabeth Mary**, dearly loved wife of **William James**, died 18th December 1984, aged 92 years.

C1-3 [spaces and mounds].

C1-4 [Plot with two iron railings missing; headstone also has lead letters missing]. In loving memory of our dear mother **Catherine Milligan**, died March 29th 1924, aged 71 years. Erected by her son and daughter, **Joseph and Catherine Jane**, Canada. Also her beloved husband **Geo. Milligan** died April 16th 1929, aged 82 years.

C1-5 [many spaces with mounds].

Colaghty Church of Ireland Cemetery

C1-6 [**ELLIS** plot]. Precious memories of our dear parents: **Willard** died 14th August 1958. **Matilda Jane** died 18th April 1993. Also their daughter **May Olive** died 26th March 1947. And granddaughter **Kathleen** died 14th May 1963.

C1-7 [space].

ROW C2

C2-1 [**MILLIGAN** plot]. In loving memory of **Thomas Andrew Milligan** (Bracklin), died 14th October 1966, aged 69 years. And his wife **Ellie** died 5th March 1980, aged 67 years. Also their son **John James (Jim)** died 5th March 2004, aged 70 years. And his wife **Mabel Evelyn** died 28th May 2012, aged 74 years.

C2-2 [spaces and mounds].

C2-3 [unmarked grave with three flower domes].

C2-4 [space and mounds].

C2-5 [Headstone]. The **SPEER** Family (Stranadarriff). **Gladys Noble** (*nee* **Cochrane**) died 15th August 1971, aged 35 years.

C2-6 [spaces and mounds].

Colaghty Church of Ireland Cemetery

C2-7 [CROZIER plot]. In loving memory of **James**, died 16th February 1982, aged 79 years. Also his wife **Mary Evelyn** died 19th November 1993, aged 80 years.

ROW C3 (Partial row starts west of the building extension; merges into C4).

C3-1 [Plot]. Cherished memories of a devoted husband and loving father **Thomas Moore**, departed this life 9th April 1965, aged 52 years. Also his beloved wife and dear mother **Blanche Elizabeth** departed this life 13th Jan. 1988, aged 68 years.

C3-2 [spaces and mounds].

ROW C4

C4-1 [KNOX plot]. In loving memory of **Margaret**, died 2nd April 1965. Her husband **Alfred** died 10th March 1981.

C4-2 [spaces and mounds].

C4-3 [Headstone with lead letters missing]. In loving memory of **Jane Woods**, died 21st November 1914, aged 81 years. Also her daughter **Elizabeth Mary Woods**, died 24th November 1912, aged 35 years. Also her brother **Hugh Marshall**, died 2nd June 1914, aged 68 years.

Colaghty Church of Ireland Cemetery

C4-4 [**WILSON** plot]. In loving memory of **Mary**, died 10th March 1916, aged 11 wks. **Arthur Mervyn** died 13th February 1940, aged 20 years. **Francis** died 18th April 1949, aged 80 years. **Mary Wilson** (*nee* **Weir**) died 8th September 1950, aged 70 years. **William** died 27th May 1958, aged 6 wks. **James (Jim)** died 19th March 1976, aged 64 years. Also his wife **Margaret (Peggy)** died 8th May 2009, aged 79 years.

C4-5 [Headstone with lead letters missing]. In loving memory of **Henry George Woods**, died 25th February 1916, aged 45 years. Also his sister **Margaret Jane Woods** died 28th July 1916, aged 38 years. And their father **Francis Woods** died 10th Jan. 1917, aged 82 years.

C4-6 [**WEIR** plot]. In loving memory of **George**, died 16th March 1978, aged 80 yrs. His loving wife **Margaret Ann** died 16th April 1979, aged 80 yrs. Their granddaughter **Helen Elizabeth Ann** died 20th Jan. 1993, aged 24 yrs. Also their son **John** died 18th July 1999, aged 71 years. And their son **Robert (George)** died 26th December 2019, aged 89 years.

C4-7 [**WILSON** plot]. (Stranadarriff*). In loving memory of **Francis (Frank)**, died 30th May 1992, aged 75 years. His son **Francis George** died 4th February 2005, aged 51 years. Also his wife **Emily** died 6th May 2013, aged 80 years.

Colaghty Church of Ireland Cemetery

C4-8 [space and mound].

C4-9 [Flower holder]. Baby **Armstrong** died 9-1-[19]84.

ROW C5

C5-1 [**MONTGOMERY** plot]. In loving memory of **George Montgomery**, died 23rd August 1969. Also his wife **Mary** died 24th September 1969. Their son **Caldwell George Montgomery** died 4th July 1992, aged 65 years.

C5-2 [space and mounds].

C5-3 [shrub].

C5-4 [space].

C5-5 [**BEATTIE** plot]. In loving memory of **Oliver** (Stranahone), died 31st May 1941, aged 70 years. His loving wife **Martha** died 16th December 1977, aged 86 years. Their son **Oliver** died 31st January 2010, aged 80 years. His wife **Sarah** died 27th December 2020, aged 82 years.

C5-6 [**WALKER** plot]. In memory of **Lily**, born 5th May 1941, died 11th October 1987, aged 46 years. Also her son **William James (Jim)** died 8th April 2005, aged 43 years, result of a road accident. [Plaque]. In loving memory of **Jim**. Always loved by **Kathleen** and **Margaret**.

Colaghty Church of Ireland Cemetery

C5-7 [JONES plot]. In loving memory of **Albert John**, died 17th Dec. 1986, aged 62 years. And his wife **Olive** died 9th April 2021, aged 97 years.

C5-8 [GINN headstone]. In loving memory of **John**, died 30th April 1990, aged 84 years. And his loving wife **Sarah Ellen** died 12th May 1996, aged 86 years.

C5-9 [space].

C5-10 [JOHNSTON plot]. In loving memory of **Annie Jane**, died 2nd December 1987, aged 89 years. Also her loving husband **William James** died 7th January 1989, aged 89 years. Re-united with their beloved daughter **Betty Wilson**, died 22nd May 1998, aged 71 years. Also her loving husband **Robert** died 27th April 2020, aged 89 years.

C5-11 [JOHNSTON plot]. In loving memory of **David**, died 13th June 1988, aged 99 years. His loving wife **Sarah Jane** died 26th October 1994, aged 88 years.

ROW C6

C6-1 [space].

C6-2 [KEYS headstone]. In loving memory of my dear father & mother. **Irvine Keys** (Glenarn) died 9th October

Colaghty Church of Ireland Cemetery

1902. **Eliza Keys** died 16th Aug. 1909. Erected by their daughter **Lizzie**, U.S.A.

C6-3 [many spaces and mounds].

C6-4 [**IRVINE** plot]. (Glassmullagh]. In loving memory of **James**, died 6th April 1929, aged 90 years. His wife **Anne** died 29th April 1924, aged 78 years. Their daughter **Margaret** died 13th July 1937, aged 70 years. Their son **William** died 23rd September 1941, aged 63 years. His wife **Minnie** died 10th July 1966, aged 81 years. Their sons: **Willie** died 8th February 1962, aged 48 years. And **Albert** died 23rd November 1982, aged 72 years. His wife **Annie** died 7th October 2016, aged 90 years.

C6-5 [**DAVIS** plot]. In loving memory of **Ellen Davis**, died 5th March 1964, aged 73 years. Also her husband **Edward** died 9th February 1971, aged 84 years.

C6-6 [**WOODS** plot]. In loving memory of **Margaret Woods**, died 18th April 1957, aged 82 years. And her husband **William** died 20th June 1958, aged 85 years. Also their daughter **Greta Crozier** died 11th November 1971, aged 63 years. And their son **Henry** died 22nd November 1989, aged 77 years. Also their son-in-law **Robert Crozier** died 27th January 1990, aged 82 years.

C6-7 [**JOHNSTON** plot]. Cherished memories of a devoted husband and loving father **William John**

(Drumbristan), departed this life 5th October 1978, aged 67 years. Also his wife **Lily** departed this life 2nd September 1998, aged 85 years. Also their son **Thomas Andrew** departed this life 18th January 2008, aged 68 years. [Plaque]. **William James Johnston** passed away 3rd November 2020, aged 82 years.

C6-8 [**CHAMBERS** plot]. In loving memory of a dear son and brother. **Wray** died 29th June 1984, aged 19 years (result of an accident). Also a dear wife and devoted mother **Margaret** died 21st November 1991, aged 61 years. Also her husband **Richard Noel** died 11th January 2003, aged 73 years.

ROW C7

C7-1 [**ARMSTRONG** plot with tall pillar; inscriptions on three sides]. In affection remembrance of **John Armstrong** who died 24th Sept.1923, aged 72. In loving memory of our dear brother **Charles** who died on Easter-day 31st March 1907. In loving memory of our dear sister **Mary Armstrong** who died 12th Nov. 1920, aged 55.

C7-2 [Huge plot]. **Capel St. George Warren Archdale**, born 22nd November 1900, died 6th October 1975, aged 74 years.

Colaghty Church of Ireland Cemetery

C7-3 [DELAP plot]. In loving memory of **William James**, died 12th February 1954, aged 60 years. His wife **Kathleen (Cassie)**, a devoted wife, mother and grandmother, died 13th November 1991, aged 67 years. Her brother **John (Jack) Hamilton** died 13th February 2003, aged 82 years.

C7-4 [ALLEN plot]. In loving memory of **Vera**, died 21st March 2001, aged 69 years.

C7-5 [VIRTUE plot]. In loving memory of **William Virtue**, died 5th Nov. 1964, aged 82 years. Also his wife **Roseleen** died 8th Nov. 1995.

C7-6 [CASSIDY plot]. In loving memory of **Elizabeth Cassidy** (Drumbristan*), died 18th August 1975, aged 83 years. Also her husband **Joe** died 6th June 1979, aged 86 years. And their daughter **Josephine (Josie)** died 19th August 2005, aged 76 years.

C7-7 [PATTERSON plot]. In loving memory of **Arthur Patterson** (Drumboarty*), died 1st August 1977.

C7-8 [PATTERSON plot]. Everlasting memories of a dear husband and loving father **Charles Patterson** (Crimlin), died 20th March 1979, aged 62 years. Also our dear son **Noel** died 2nd Sept. 1978, aged 27 years. And a loving wife and mother **Agnes** who died 27th January 2000, aged 78 years. Also our dear son and brother **Ivan** died 31st May 2018, aged 60 years.

C7-9 [**WEIR** plot; inscription rearranged for clarity]. In loving memory of a dear mother **Gretta** (*nee* **Muldoon**), died 19th June 1988, aged 41 years.

C7-10 [space].

SECTION D

ROW D1

D1-1 [space].

D1-2 [**JOHNSTON** plot]. In loving memory of **Margaret Jane Johnston** (Drumnavahan*), died 21st January 1974, aged 67 years. Also **Mary Johnston** died 15th June 1937, aged 70 years. And her husband **William Johnston** died 23rd May 1944, aged 82 years. Also **William John Johnston**, husband of **Margaret J.**, died 24th January 1989, aged 90 years.

D1-3 [**CROZIER** plot with headstone and four perimeter inscriptions]. In loving memory of my dear husband **Francis Christopher Crozier** who departed this life 10th Jany. 1936, aged 40 years. Also his father **Thomas**

Colaghty Church of Ireland Cemetery

Crozier who departed this life 2nd May 1927, aged 74 years. Also **Helen P. Crozier**, wife of **Francis Christopher**, who departed this life 26th September 1978, aged 72 years. **Muriel Winifred Crozier**, daughter of **Francis C. Crozier** and **Helen P. Crozier**, who departed this life 12th March 2019, aged 86 years. [Perimeter]. **Mary J. Crozier** died 26th March 1941, aged 75 years. **William J. Crozier** died 7th June 1945, aged 60 years. Also his wife **Elizabeth M. Crozier** died 5th July 1976, aged 86 years. **William Francis Crozier** died 14th July 2007, aged 81 years.

D1-4 [space].

D1-5 [Plot with horizontal iron railings]. In loving memory of **William John Irvine** of Stranadarriff* who died 19th December 1927, aged 73 years. **Anne Jane** died 12th Dec. 1955, aged 91 years. **Louise Frances** died 25th Feb. 1957, aged 63 years. **John James** died 12th Jan. 1976, aged 12 years. **William** died 1st April 1978, aged 80 years. **Robert Henry (Bobby)** died 27th July 1982, aged 47 years.

D1-6 [**GINN** plot]. In loving memory of our dear son **William James**, died 15th November 1956, aged 9 years. And his mother **Barbara Jane** died 18th January 1981, aged 69 years. Also her husband **Crozier** died 9th February 1991, aged 87 years. And their son **Robert John** died 16th

67

Colaghty Church of Ireland Cemetery

July 2002, aged 52 years. Also their son **Edward George** died 6th May 2019, aged 67 years.

D1-7 [space].

D1-8 [**WALKER** plot with five **VIRTUE** perimeter inscriptions]. In loving memory of **Robert John Walker** (Mweelbane), died 12th July 1968, aged 72 years. Also his wife **Mary Jane Walker** died 30th May 1983, aged 87 years. Also their son **William James (Jim)** died 3rd July 2009, aged 74 years. [Perimeter]. **John Virtue** died 24th Nov. 1934, aged 79 years. **Mary Jane Virtue** died 12th March 1928, aged 63 years. **James Virtue** died 3rd Oct. 1937, aged 46 years. **Jack Virtue** died 25th March 1960, aged 62 years. **William Virtue** died 29th Aug. 1947, aged 59 years.

D1-9 [**BOYD** plot]. (Greenan [Tyrone]). In loving memory of **Matilda Ann Boyd**, died 2nd November 1928. Her husband **James** died 18th January 1937. Their daughter **Kathleen** died 4th March 1991. And their son **Thomas** died 6th December 1992.

D1-10 [**BEST** headstone]. In loving memory of our father **Matthew Best,** J.P., died 29th December 1967, aged 77 years. And our mother **Henrietta Best** died 13th February 1976, aged 81 years. Also son **Matthew (Harry) Best** died 2nd April 1993, aged 70 years. And his wife **Maureen**

Colaghty Church of Ireland Cemetery

Maude died 30th May 2021, aged 89 years. Erected by **Mary, Harry** and **Noel**.

D1-11 [**VIRTUE** plot]. In loving memory of a dear husband, father and grandad, **Robert George (Bobby)** born 11th September 1918, died 15th November 2000.

ROW D2

D2-1 [space].

D2-2 [**BRATTON** headstone]. In loving memory of **Oliver James**, born 4th May 1904, died on 15th June 1989. Also his wife **Sarah Anne**, born 20th June 1920, died on 23rd May 1991.

D2-3 [**BRATTON** partial plot]. In loving memory of a dear husband and father **Samuel George**, died 7th November 1990, aged 65 years. A dear wife, mother, grandmother and great-grandmother **Elizabeth Margaret Jane (Beth)** died 4th July 2022, aged 89 years.

D2-4 [**BRATTON** headstone]. In loving memory of **William Robert Joseph**, died 9th November 1993, aged 76 years. And his sister **Margaret Elizabeth** died 19th November 1996, aged 76 years.

D2-5 [spaces].

Colaghty Church of Ireland Cemetery

D2-6 [**GINN** headstone]. In loving memory of **Edward**, died 23rd January 2013, aged 80 years. Also his beloved wife **Sarah Jane (Sally)** died 18th April 2021, aged 87 years.

D2-7 [**EVANS** flower holder].

D2-8 [Flower holder]. Precious memories of a dear Mum **Kathleen McCaskie**.

D2-9 [space and depression].

D2-10 [**VIRTUE** partial plot]. Cherished memories of a dear son and brother **John Wesley**, died 20th January 2016, aged 31 years.

D2-11 [**CURTIS** partial plot]. In loving memory of **Sarah Jane (Sally)**, devoted wife, mother and nana, 31st Oct. 1944 – 12th Feb. 2016.

D2-12 [**MARTIN** partial plot]. In loving memory of a dear wife, mother and grandmother **Arvina Annabella (Ivy)**, died 31st March 2016, aged 84 years. Also a dear husband, father and grandfather **John James**, died 15th February 2019, aged 87 years.

Colaghty Church of Ireland Cemetery

ROW D3

D3-1 [**BEACOMBE** headstone]. In loving memory of **Robert Irvine**, died 4th June 1998, aged 82 years.

D3-2 [**GINN** headstone]. Precious and lovely memories of a beloved husband and father **Gordon Edward**, died 28th June 1998, aged 40 years.

D3-3 [**CURTIS** partial plot]. In loving memory of a dear husband and father **William J.C. Curtis**, died 10th February 1998. Also a beloved wife and mother **Irene Mary Curtis** died 9th June 2010.

D3-4 [**WALKER** partial plot]. In loving memory of **Irvine Johnston**, died 7th June 1994, aged 64 years. Also his beloved wife **Mary Valerie** died 3rd November 2018, aged 80 years.

D3-5 [space].

D3-6 [**IRVINE** book-shaped marker]. In loving memory of baby **Adam**, 1-8-[20]09.

D3-7 [spaces].

D3-8 [**ELLIS** flower holder].

D3-9 [spaces].

Colaghty Church of Ireland Cemetery

D3-10 [Flower holder for baby burial]. Born an angel. **Harley Mason Johnston**, 09-11-2011.

D3-11 [space].

D3-12 [**JOHNSTON** partial plot]. In loving memory of **William (Sonny)**, died 9th October 2011, aged 88 years. Also his brother **Thomas (Tommy)** died 29th August 2013, aged 88 years. And their sister **Ellen** died 13th May 2016, aged 96 years. [Flower holder indicates their townland as Gushedy].

D3-13 [**WOODS** partial plot]. In loving memory of a devoted husband and father **Thomas Anthony**, died 16th February 2012, aged 50 years.

D3-14 [**ARMSTRONG** partial plot]. (Stranahone). In loving memory of **George Nixon (Geordie)**, died 14th July 2014, aged 78 years.

ROW D4

D4-1 [**SCANLON** partial plot]. Precious and loving memories of our dear son and brother **Alistair Samuel**, died tragically 24th October 1998, aged 19 years. Devoted husband and father **James Joseph** died suddenly 5th January 2001, aged 60 years. Devoted wife, mother and

Colaghty Church of Ireland Cemetery

grandmother **Elizabeth Margaret Scanlon** (*nee* **Foster**), died 15th September 2013, aged 65 years.

D4-2 [**JOHNSTON** partial plot]. (Stranadarriff*). In loving memory of a devoted husband, father and grandfather **William John (Jack)**, died 26th November 1998, aged 75 years.

D4-3 [**WALKER** headstone]. In loving memory of **David Godfrey**, died 27th October 2002, aged 78 years.

D4-4 [**MILLEN** headstone]. In loving memory of a dear mother **Lily (Robinson)**, died 20th January 2009, aged 96 years. **MACK, Sidney (Robinson)** died 7th April 2014, aged 99 years. A beloved mother, grandmother and a sister of **Lily**.

D4-5 [space].

D4-6 [**IRVINE** partial plot]. (Stranadarriff*). In loving memory of a dear husband, father and grandfather **William John (Willie)**, died 24th November 2003, aged 74 years.

D4-7 [**VANCE** partial plot]. In loving memory of a dear son and brother **Thomas Joseph**, died 7th February 2004, aged 18 years. (Result of an accident).

D4-8 [**VIRTUE** partial plot]. Cherished memories of a loving husband and devoted father. **David** passed away 17th December 2004, aged 46 years.

D4-9 [**JOHNSTON** partial plot]. In loving memory of **Thomas Albert**, died 13th August 2006, aged 80 years. Also his wife **Annie Eileen** died 10th February 2009, aged 77 years.

D4-10 [**ELLIS** partial plot with book-shaped tribute]. In loving memory of a dear husband and father **Matthew John**, died 20th October 2007, aged 79 years. Also a dear wife and devoted mother **Sarah Kathleen**, died 9th December 2012, aged 81 years. [Book-shaped pedestal marker]. From son **Robert**, **Louise** and grandchildren.

D4-11 [**IRVINE** partial plot]. In loving memory of a dear husband and father **William James** (Kilsmullan*), died 19th July 2009, aged 82 years.

D4-12 [**ELLIS** headstone]. (Monavreece*). In loving memory of **William David**, died 7th November 2013, aged 73 years.

SECTION E (Rows starting against west wall).

ROW E1

Colaghty Church of Ireland Cemetery

E1-1 [**IRWIN** partial plot]. In loving memory of a dear wife, mother, and grandmother **Isobel**, died 7th April 2016, aged 59 years.

E1-2 [**KILFEDDER** partial plot]. In loving memory of **Albert John**, died 15th October 2016, aged 74 years.

E1-3 [**JOHNSTON** partial plot]. In loving memory of our dear son and brother **David William Geoffrey**, died 25th November 2017, aged 37 years. Also his father **Thomas Geoffrey** died 13th April 2018, aged 87 years.

E1-4 [Flower holder]. Baby **Seth Goldie**, 3rd April 2018.

E1-5 spaces].

ROW E2

E2-1 [**WOODS** partial plot]. In loving memory of **William Ernest**, died 6th November 2019, aged 76 years.

E2-2 [**THOMPSON** partial plot]. In loving memory of a dear husband, father and grandfather **William John (Jack)**, died 11th December 2020, aged 78 years.

E2-3 [**DURAND** partial plot]. In loving memory of a dear wife, mother and grandmother **Alice Florence**, died 25th December 2020, aged 86 years.

E2-4 [**FOSTER** partial plot]. In loving memory of a dear husband, father and grandfather **William (Ernest)**, died 7th November 2021, aged 81 years.

E2-5 [**KILFEDDER** partial plot]. (Drumconnis, Ballinamallard). In loving memory of a dear wife **Sylvia** *(nee Telford)*, 8th August 1948—13th April 2022.

E2-6 [**EWING** partial plot]. Precious memories of **Robert James (Bobby)**, loving husband, father and Granda, passed away 22nd April 2022, aged 80 years.

ROW E3

E3-1 [Temporary marker]. **John Johnston** died 18th October 2022.

Section M : Memorials

M-1 [Plaque on wall on inside of east gate]. Gate gifted by **Elizabeth** and **Cheryl Keys** in memory of their grandfather **Samuel Keys** (Glenarn), 2018.

M-2 [Bench along north wall of cemetery at end of Row C2]. Colaghty Parish Church, 175th Anniversary. Bench

Colaghty Church of Ireland Cemetery

presented by **David, Sandra Milligan** & Family, 2019. [There is also a duplicate memorial bench on the north side of the church presented by the same family.]

Tirwinny Methodist Cemetery

Transcriptions of Tirwinny Methodist Tombstones

SECTION A

Row A1

A1-1 [spaces]

A1-2 [**McCLAUGHRY** plot; no names] (Leehan).

A1-3 [spaces].

A1-4 [Plot]. In loving memory of **John James Johnston**, died 9th June 1910, aged 56 years. Also his wife **Elizabeth Jane** died 8th May 1932, aged 80 years. Their son **Thomas** died 4th March 1950, aged 66 years. And daughter **Isabella** died 5th December 1964, aged 71 years.

A1-5 [**ARMSTRONG** plot]. In loving memory of **Robert**, beloved son of **Nixon** and **Eliza Anne Armstrong** (Movarran*), died 10th July 1933, aged 33 years. His mother **Eliza Anne** died 11th Nov. 1950, aged 78 years. His father **Nixon** died 2nd Feb. 1955, aged 89 years. Their beloved son **Wm. John** died 6th Sept. 1965, aged 78 years. His wife **Mary Jane** died 6th June 1991, aged 84 years.

Tirwinny Methodist Cemetery

[entrance sidewalk]

ROW A2

A2-1 [spaces].

A2-32 [Plot]. In loving memory of **James Samuel Weir**, died 24th May 1947, aged 52 years. His wife **Mary Ellen** died 20th July 1930, aged 35 years. Her son **Alexander Dalton** died 24th January 1977, aged 54 years. And his wife **Sadie** died 25th February 2005, aged 83 years.

A2-3 [**KNOX** plot]. In grateful memory of **Francis Knox**, J.P., (Drumsawna* House, Ederney), who died 20th June 1932, aged 82 years. Also his wife **Mary Annie** who died 22nd June 1943, aged 79 years.

A2-4 [spaces to entrance sidewalk].

ROW A3

A3-1 [spaces].

A3-2 [**MARSHALL** plot]. In loving memory of **Frank H. Marshall** (evangelist), called home 11th August 1982. Also his loving wife **Violet** called home 9th January 1993.

A3-3 [**JOHNSTON** plot]. In loving memory of **Robert Johnston** (Tirmacspird*), who died 2nd July 1928, aged 69 years. Also his wife **Catherine** who died 13th September 1946, aged 73 years.

A3-4 [spaces to church].

ROW A4

A4-1 [spaces].

A4-2 [**WALKER** plot with headstone, plaque and flower holder]. In loving memory of our dear parents: **Andrew James** (Mweelbane*) died 29th September 1984, aged 81 years. His wife **Margaret Jane** died 3rd July 1996, aged 72 years. [Plaque]. Treasured memories of Mum & Dad. Always cherished by son **Cyril** and family. [Flower holder]. In loving memory of Mum & Dad. Always remembered by son **Harold**.

A4-3 [Plot with low iron rails]. In loving memory of our dear mother **Anne Jane Walker** (Meenmossogue*) who died 18th March 1928, aged 84 years. Erected by her daughter **Tillie J. Walker**.

Tirwinny Methodist Cemetery

ROW A5

A5-1 [spaces].

A5-2 [Plot]. In loving memory of **James Johnston** (Mweelbane*) who died 28th Feb. 1930, aged 79 years. Also his wife **Margaret** who died 24th Dec. 1919, aged 68 years. And their son **William** who died 7th July 1931, aged 55 years. Also his wife **Mary** who died 3rd Feb. 1950, aged 88 years.

A5-3 [space].

ROW A6

A6-1 [spaces].

A6-2 [**BARTON** plot]. In memory of our parents: **Mary E. Barton** died September 26th 1927. **Adam Barton** died December 18th 1937. Also our brother **Ernest C. Barton** died March 7th 1938.

A6-3 [space].

A6-4 [**COLVIN** plot]. In loving memory of **Thomas**, died 17th November 1933. His wife **Sarah** died 12th April 1966. Their son **Thomas** died on 26th October 1980, aged 85 years.

ROW A7

A7-1 spaces].

A7-2 [JOHNSTON plot with low railings]. In memory of my beloved uncle and aunt: **James Johnston** who died 23rd Nov. 1922, aged 81 years. Also his wife **Eliza** who died 25th Sept. 1928, aged 62 years.

A7-3 [spaces].

ROW A8

A8-1 [spaces].

A8-2 [MONAGHAN plot]. In loving memory of **David Claude**, died 12th June 1999, aged 69 years.

A8-3 [Plot with broken headstone and pedestal marker]. **Lily Monaghan** died 19th November 2016.

A8-4 [JOHNSTON plot]. In loving memory of **Hilray Olwyn** who died 9th June 1991, aged 19 years. Lovely and beautiful in her short life.

A8-5 [MONAGHAN plot]. In loving memory of **Thomas**, died 24th February 1984. Also his wife **Jenny** died 11th February 1985. And their daughter **Isabella** died 21st April 2013.

Tirwinny Methodist Cemetery

SECTION B

Row B1

B1-1 [**MOFFITT** headstone]. Treasured memories of **Elizabeth**, died 5th November 1901, aged 23 years. **George** died 9th September 1933, aged 58 years. **Susan** died 7th March 1952, aged 81 years. **Thomas** died 4th December 1954, aged 85 years. **Robert** died 22nd December 1961, aged 77 years. **Annie** wife of **George** died 3rd May 1968, aged 71 years. **Thomas Andrew** son of **George** and **Annie** died 6th November 2003, aged 84 years. **Mary Jane** wife of **Thomas Andrew** died 14th January 2017, aged 92 years.

B1-2 [space].

B1-3 [**MOFFITT** plot]. In loving memory of our dear father **Edward Moffitt**, passed away 26th October 1933. And our dear mother **Ellen** passed away 20th November 1952.

B1-4 [many spaces].

B1-5 [**JOHNSTON** plot]. In loving memory of **William Edward Johnston** (Lack) who died 10th January 1937, aged 86 years. Also his wife **Rebecca** who died 14th March 1955, aged 90 years. And their son **William Robert** who died 8th October 1967, aged 77 years. And daughter **Evelyn Martha** who died 21st May 1978, aged 81 years.

B1-6 **[CHITTICK** plot]. In loving memory of our dear parents: **William** died 8th August 1942, aged 78 years. **Elizabeth** died 15th Jan. 1961, aged 92 years. Daughter **Hennie** died 28th November 1943, aged 25 years.

B1-7 [Plot]. In loving memory of **Mary Jane Johnston** (Stranadarriff*), died 20th November 1944, aged 74 years and was interred here. Also her mother **Margaret** died 25th June 1917, aged 74 years. And her father **John** died 17th May 1927, aged 84 years and were interred in Colaghty Churchyard.

B1-8 [spaces].

ROW B2

B2-1 [space].

B2-2 [**MOFFITT** headstone]. Treasured memories of a dear wife and mother **Martha Isabel**, passed away 10th June 2010, aged 79 years. Also dearly beloved son **William George** passed away 6th September 2016, aged 53 years.

B2-3 [**SIMPSON** plot]. (Ederney). In loving memory of our dear parents: **Sadie** who died 13th November 1971. **James** who died 16th April 1977. Their son **Victor**

James, who died 19th August 2015, a much loved husband, father and grandfather.

B2-4 [JOHNSTON plot]. In loving memory of **Arthur Johnston** (Glasmullagh), died 2nd June 1906, aged 58 years. Also his wife **Sarah Ann** died 17th January 1951, aged 90 years. Also son **Arthur** died 24th August 1972, aged 85 years. Also son **Robert Ernest** died 13th April 1976, aged 71 years. Also his wife **Annie Prior** died 10th May 1982, aged 75 years. And son **Arthur Eric** died 2nd Nov. 1992, aged 55 yrs.

B2-5 [Plot with low iron railing]. In loving memory of my dear husband **Thomas N. Glendinning** who departed this life 15th April 1955, aged 75 years. His wife **Margaret** who departed this life 27th Oct. 1979, aged 89 years.

B2-6 [**MULDOON** plot]. In memory of the **Muldoon** family (Corlaght* East), erected 1961.

B2-7 [spaces].

ROW B3

B3-1 [space].

Tirwinny Methodist Cemetery

B3-2 [JOHNSON plot]. In loving memory of **Charles John**, died 18th March 1995, aged 77 years. Also his wife **Isabella Ann** died 18th September 2015, aged 95 years.

B3-3 [JOHNSON plot]. In loving memory of **Jervis Johnson**, died 25th February 1973, aged 83 years. Also his wife **Elizabeth** died 2nd March 1991, aged 100 years. And their son **Arthur** died 12th December 1996, aged 82 years. Also their daughter **Dorothy** died 2nd March 2009, aged 88 years.

B3-4 [BARTON plot]. In loving memory of a dear husband and father **Oliver**, died 2nd Feb. 1973, aged 63 years. Also his wife **Margaret**, a devoted mother, died 7th Feb. 2017, aged 97 years. (Meenmossogue*).

B3-5 [spaces].

ROW B4 [Empty]

ROW B5

B5-1 [spaces].

B5-2 [SIMPSON headstone]. In loving memory of **Frederick John (Freddie)**, a loving husband & father, died 13th October 2012, aged 78 years.

Tirwinny Methodist Cemetery

B5-3 [**THOMPSON** plot]. In loving memory of **Sadie**, died 11th October 2003, aged 61 years. And her husband **Freddie** died 31st January 2016, aged 75 years.

Key to the Index of Names

Each person mentioned on the gravestones has been included in the index. This might result in a person being listed more than once in the index because they might have erected a monument for a family member, but were buried under another one. Each person's name has been keyed to his/her location in the cemetery; for example, A2-3, meaning A section, Row 2, plot or headstone number 3. When a woman has been identified as married, her surname has been *italicized*.

Because we have combined the indexes of both cemeteries we have given the tombstones from Tirwinny Methodist Cemetery a TM prefix, for example TM-B1-5.

You will find on the tombstones that there are inconsistencies in the spelling of forenames and surnames, even on the same stone. For example, McElroy might also be spelled McIlroy, McKilroy, McGilroy, etc. It is important to look at variations of spellings to find possible ancestors.

Index of Names and Locations

	A	B	C	D
1	**Surname**	**Names**	**Death**	**Location**
2	Acheson	Evelyn	1944	A6-1
3	Acheson	George	1947	A6-1
4	Acheson	Margaret	1952	A6-1
5	Acheson	William	1984	A6-1
6	Acheson	William Henry	1897	A4-1
7	Acheson	Wm.		A4-1
8	Allen	Vera	2001	C7-4
9	Archdale	Capel St. George W.	1975	C7-2
10	Armstrong	Charles	1907	C7-1
11	*Armstrong*	Eliza Anne	1950	TM-A1-5
12	Armstrong	George Nixon	2014	D3-14
13	Armstrong	John	1923	C7-1
14	*Armstrong*	Margaret Jane	1998	A16-1
15	Armstrong	Mary	1920	C7-1
16	*Armstrong*	Mary Jane	1991	TM-A1-5
17	Armstrong	Nixon	1955	TM-A1-5
18	Armstrong	Robert	1933	TM-A1-5
19	Armstrong	Thomas James	1992	A16-1
20	Armstrong	Wm. John	1965	TM-A1-5
21	Armstrong		1984	C4-9
22	Barton	Adam	1937	TM-A6-2
23	Barton	Andrew	1981	A7-3
24	Barton	Andrew	1885	B5-6
25	*Barton*	Ann	2007	A7-3
26	*Barton*	Anne Jane	1884	A7-2
27	Barton	Bill		A7-2
28	Barton	Caldwell		A7-2
29	Barton	Daisy		A7-2
30	*Barton*	Dinah		A7-2
31	Barton	Ernest C.	1938	TM-A6-2
32	Barton	George		A7-2
33	Barton	Ida		A7-2

Index of Names and Locations

	A	B	C	D
1	**Surname**	**Names**	**Death**	**Location**
34	Barton	Maggie	1893	A16-2
35	*Barton*	Margaret	2017	TM-B3-4
36	Barton	Martha		A7-2
37	*Barton*	Mary E.	1927	TM-A6-2
38	Barton	Mervyn		A7-2
39	Barton	Noll		A7-2
40	Barton	Oliver	1973	TM-B3-4
41	Barton	William		A16-2
42	Barton	William John	1945	A7-2
43	Beacom	Albert	1990	A18-1
44	Beacom	Elizabeth Jane	1973	B2-8
45	Beacom	Joseph	1986	B2-8
46	*Beacom*	Violet Maud	1985	A18-1
47	Beacom	William James K.	1961	B2-8
48	Beacome	Robert Irvine	1998	D3-1
49	*Beattie*	Elizabeth Jane	1952	B7-9
50	*Beattie*	Martha	1977	C5-5
51	Beattie	Oliver Jr.	2010	C5-5
52	Beattie	Oliver Sr.	1941	C5-5
53	*Beattie*	Sarah	2020	C5-5
54	Beattie	William	1936	B7-9
55	*Best*	Harry		D1-10
56	*Best*	Henrietta	1976	D1-10
57	Best	Mary		D1-10
58	Best	Matthew	1967	D1-10
59	Best	Matthew (Harry)	1993	D1-10
60	*Best*	Maureen Maude	2021	D1-10
61	Best	Noel		D1-10
62	Boyd	James	1937	D1-9
63	Boyd	Kathleen	1991	D1-9
64	*Boyd*	Matilda Ann	1928	D1-9
65	Boyd	Thomas	1992	D1-9

Index of Names and Locations

	A	B	C	D
1	Surname	Names	Death	Location
66	Bratton	Elizabeth	1941	A18-2
67	Bratton	Elizabeth Margaret J.	2022	D2-3
68	Bratton	George	1973	A13-1
69	Bratton	Margaret Elizabeth	1996	D2-4
70	Bratton	Margaret Maria	1979	A13-1
71	Bratton	Oliver James	1989	D2-2
72	Bratton	Robert	1965	A18-2
73	Bratton	Samuel George	1990	D2-3
74	Bratton	Samuel Thomas	1953	A18-2
75	Bratton	Sarah Anne	1991	D2-2
76	Bratton	Sarah Jane	1961	A18-2
77	Bratton	William	1947	A18-2
78	Bratton	William Robert J.	1993	D2-4
79	Brown	Clive	1994	B4-14
80	Brown	Dorothy Rose Eliza.	1997	B4-14
81	Brown	Edward James	1971	B4-14
82	Brown	Harriett May	2011	B1-7
83	Brown	Jacob	1971	B1-7
84	Brown	Margaret	1967	B4-14
85	Brown	Mary	1967	B1-7
86	Buchanan	Mary	1986	A1-1
87	Buchanan	Robert	1973	A1-1
88	Caldwell	Elizabeth	1959	A9-3
89	Caldwell	William John	1939	A9-3
90	Cassidy	Elizabeth	1975	C7-6
91	Cassidy	Joe	1979	C7-6
92	Cassidy	Josephine (Josie)	2005	C7-6
93	Chambers	Margaret	1991	C6-8
94	Chambers	Richard Noel	2003	C6-8
95	Chambers	Wray	1984	C6-8
96	Chittick	Elizabeth	1961	TM-B1-6
97	Chittick	Hennie	1943	TM-B1-6

Index of Names and Locations

	A	B	C	D
1	**Surname**	**Names**	**Death**	**Location**
98	Chittick	William	1942	TM-B1-6
99	Colvin	Sarah	1966	TM-A6-4
100	Colvin	Thomas	1933	TM-A6-4
101	Colvin	Thomas	1980	TM-A6-4
102	Crozier	Annie Jane	1963	A9-2
103	Crozier	Charles	1966	A9-2
104	Crozier	Elizabeth	1956	B1-3
105	Crozier	Elizabeth	1902	B1-3
106	Crozier	Elizabeth M.	1976	D1-3
107	Crozier	Francis	1934	A9-2
108	Crozier	Francis Christopher	1936	D1-3
109	Crozier	Georgina Mabel	1985	B1-3
110	Crozier	Greta	1971	C6-6
111	Crozier	Helen P.	1978	D1-3
112	Crozier	James	1982	C2-7
113	Crozier	John	1942	B1-3
114	Crozier	John	1985	B1-3
115	Crozier	Margaret	1915	A9-2
116	Crozier	Mary Evelyn	1993	C2-7
117	Crozier	Mary J.	1941	D1-3
118	Crozier	Muriel Winifred	2019	D1-3
119	Crozier	Robert	1990	C6-6
120	Crozier	Thomas	1927	D1-3
121	Crozier	William	1966	B1-3
122	Crozier	William Francis	2007	D1-3
123	Crozier	William J.	1945	D1-3
124	Curtis	Anne	1992	B3-1
125	Curtis	Brian	1960	B3-1
126	Curtis	Fred	1984	B3-1
127	Curtis	Irene Mary	2010	D3-3
128	Curtis	Sarah Jane (Sally)	2016	D2-11
129	Curtis	William J.C.	1998	D3-3

Index of Names and Locations

	A	B	C	D
1	**Surname**	**Names**	**Death**	**Location**
130	Cuzner	Anna Elizabeth	2010	A10-2
131	Davis	Edward	1971	C6-5
132	Davis	Ellen	1964	C6-5
133	Davis	Henry		B6-1
134	Davis	Mary	1876	B6-1
135	Davis	Mary	1938	B6-8
136	Davis	Mary Jane	1892	A8-1
137	Davis	William	1876	B6-1
138	Davis	William Jr.	1907	B6-8
139	Davis	William Sr.	1941	B6-8
140	Delap	Kathleen (Cassie)	1991	C7-3
141	Delap	William James	1954	C7-3
142	Durand	Alice Florence	2020	E2-3
143	Ellis	Kathleen	1963	C1-6
144	Ellis	Louise		D4-10
145	Ellis	Matilda Jane	1993	C1-6
146	Ellis	Matthew John	2007	D4-10
147	Ellis	May Olive	1947	C1-6
148	Ellis	Robert		D4-10
149	Ellis	Sarah Kathleen	2012	D4-10
150	Ellis	Willard	1958	C1-6
151	Ellis	William David	2013	D4-12
152	Ellis			D3-8
153	Emery	Alexander	1924	B2-4
154	Emery	Elizabeth	1940	B2-4
155	Emery	Matilda	1947	B2-4
156	Emery	Sarah	1917	B2-4
157	Evans	Elizabeth Catherine	1961	B3-6
158	Evans	Emily Rebecca	1989	B7-10
159	Evans	George	1924	B3-6
160	Evans	George	1998	B3-6
161	Evans	George Stewart	1947	B3-6

Index of Names and Locations

	A	B	C	D
1	**Surname**	**Names**	**Death**	**Location**
162	Evans	Mary Jane	1914	B3-6
163	Evans	Oliver	1942	B7-10
164	Evans	William Andrew	1991	B7-10
165	Evans			D2-7
166	Ewing	Robert James (Bobby)	2022	E2-6
167	Farrell	Abraham		B7-6
168	Foster	Elizabeth Mary	2001	B1-4
169	Foster	George Hamilton	2005	B1-4
170	Foster	Kim		B1-4
171	Foster	Percy	2020	B1-4
172	Foster	Robert Victor	1945	B1-4
173	Foster	William (Ernest)	2021	E2-4
174	Gilmour	Ivy Gladys	1983	B2-2
175	Gilmour	James	1974	B2-2
176	Gilmour	Minnie	1961	A6-3
177	Gilmour	Robert Ferguson	1993	B2-2
178	Gilmour	Sarah Jane	1958	B2-2
179	Gilmour	William James	1973	B2-2
180	Ginn	Barbara Jane	1981	D1-6
181	Ginn	Crozier	1991	D1-6
182	Ginn	Edward	2013	D2-6
183	Ginn	Edward George	2019	D1-6
184	Ginn	Gordon Edward	1998	D3-2
185	Ginn	John	1990	C5-8
186	Ginn	Robert John	2002	D1-6
187	Ginn	Sarah Ellen	1996	C5-8
188	Ginn	Sarah Jane (Sally)	2021	D2-6
189	Ginn	William James	1956	D1-6
190	Glendinning	Margaret	1979	TM-B2-5
191	Glendinning	Thomas N.	1955	TM-B2-5
192	Goddard	Annie	1981	B1-10
193	Goldie	Seth	2018	E1-4

	A	B	C	D
1	**Surname**	**Names**	**Death**	**Location**
194	Graham	Jane	2001	B7-7
195	Graham	Joan Kathleen	2000	B7-7
196	Graham	John James (Jim)	1994	B7-7
197	Hall	Sarah Mary	1943	B6-2
198	Hall	William Whitcombe	1931	B6-2
199	Hamilton	John (Jack)	2003	C7-3
200	Hicks	Elizabeth Mary	1984	C1-2
201	Hicks	Robert James	1981	C1-2
202	Hicks	William James	1943	C1-2
203	Hughes	Margaret Isobella	2005	B5-8
204	Hughes	Norman Addison	2000	B5-8
205	Hughes	William John	1992	B5-8
206	Ingram	James	1960	B6-4
207	Ingram	Mary Jane	1959	B6-4
208	Irvine	Adam	2009	D3-6
209	Irvine	Albert	1982	C6-4
210	Irvine	Anne	1924	C6-4
211	Irvine	Anne Jane	1955	D1-5
212	Irvine	Annie	2016	C6-4
213	Irvine	Ethel Mary Ruth	1966	B2-7
214	Irvine	Ida	1982	B2-7
215	Irvine	James	1929	C6-4
216	Irvine	John James	1969	B2-11
217	Irvine	John James	1976	D1-5
218	Irvine	Louise Frances	1957	D1-5
219	Irvine	Margaret	1967	B2-11
220	Irvine	Margaret	1937	C6-4
221	Irvine	Minnie	1966	C6-4
222	Irvine	Robert H.	1979	B2-7
223	Irvine	Robert Henry	2000	B2-11
224	Irvine	Robert Henry (Bobby)	1982	D1-5
225	Irvine	William	1941	C6-4

Index of Names and Locations

	A	B	C	D
1	Surname	Names	Death	Location
226	Irvine	William	1978	D1-5
227	Irvine	William James	2009	D4-11
228	Irvine	William John	1927	D1-5
229	Irvine	William John (Willie)	2003	D4-6
230	Irvine	Willie	1962	C6-4
231	Irwin	Isobel	2016	E1-1
232	Johnson	Arthur	1996	TM-B3-3
233	Johnson	Charles John	1995	TM-B3-2
234	Johnson	Dorothy	2009	TM-B3-3
235	Johnson	Elizabeth	1991	TM-B3-3
236	Johnson	Isabella Ann	2015	TM-B3-2
237	Johnson	Jervis	1973	TM-B3-3
238	Johnston	Annie Eileen	2021	B1-2
239	Johnston	Annie Eileen	2009	D4-9
240	Johnston	Annie Elizabeth	1938	B2-6
241	Johnston	Annie Jane	1987	C5-10
242	Johnston	Annie Prior	1982	TM-B2-4
243	Johnston	Arthur	1906	TM-B2-4
244	Johnston	Arthur	1972	TM-B2-4
245	Johnston	Arthur Eric	1992	TM-B2-4
246	Johnston	Catherine	1946	TM-A3-3
247	Johnston	Chadwalder Blaney	1974	B2-6
248	Johnston	Charles		A8-2
249	Johnston	David	1991	B5-10
250	Johnston	David	1988	C5-11
251	Johnston	David William Geoffrey	2017	E1-3
252	Johnston	Dorothy (Dora)	1994	B3-9
253	Johnston	Eliza	1928	TM-A7-2
254	Johnston	Elizabeth	2011	A6-3
255	Johnston	Elizabeth	1940	B1-4
256	Johnston	Elizabeth	1936	B5-10
257	Johnston	Elizabeth Jane	1932	TM-A1-4

Index of Names and Locations

	A	B	C	D
1	**Surname**	**Names**	**Death**	**Location**
258	Johnston	Ellen	2016	D3-12
259	Johnston	Evelyn Martha	1978	TM-B1-5
260	Johnston	Gary	1975	A5-2
261	Johnston	Harley Mason	2011	D3-10
262	Johnston	Hilray Olwyn	1991	TM-A8-4
263	Johnston	Isabella	1988	A5-2
264	Johnston	Isabella	1964	TM-A1-4
265	Johnston	James	1922	TM-A7-2
266	Johnston	James	1930	TM-A5-2
267	Johnston	James (Jim)	1965	A6-3
268	Johnston	John	2022	E3-1
269	Johnston	John	1927	TM-B1-7
270	Johnston	John James	1910	TM-A1-4
271	Johnston	Joseph	1967	A5-2
272	Johnston	Kathleen	1895	A8-2
273	Johnston	Kenneth	2011	A8-2
274	Johnston	Lily	1962	B5-10
275	Johnston	Lily	1998	C6-7
276	Johnston	Margaret	1910	A8-2
277	Johnston	Margaret	1917	TM-B1-7
278	Johnston	Margaret	1919	TM-A5-2
279	Johnston	Margaret Jane	1972	B2-6
280	Johnston	Margaret Jane	1974	D1-2
281	Johnston	Mary	1937	D1-2
282	Johnston	Mary	1950	TM-A5-2
283	Johnston	Mary Jane	1944	TM-B1-7
284	Johnston	Norah	1969	A5-2
285	Johnston	Rebecca	1955	TM-B1-5
286	Johnston	Robert	1985	A8-2
287	Johnston	Robert	1970	B3-9
288	Johnston	Robert	1928	TM-A3-3
289	Johnston	Robert (Bob)	1966	A6-3

Index of Names and Locations

	A	B	C	D
1	**Surname**	**Names**	**Death**	**Location**
290	Johnston	Robert Ernest	1976	TM-B2-4
291	Johnston	Robert James	1985	B1-2
292	Johnston	Samuel S.		B2-6
293	*Johnston*	Sarah Ann	1951	TM-B2-4
294	*Johnston*	Sarah Jane	1969	B1-2
295	*Johnston*	Sarah Jane	1994	C5-11
296	Johnston	Thomas	1928	B2-6
297	Johnston	Thomas	1924	B5-10
298	Johnston	Thomas	1950	TM-A1-4
299	Johnston	Thomas (Tommy)	2013	D3-12
300	Johnston	Thomas Albert	2006	D4-9
301	Johnston	Thomas Andrew	2008	C6-7
302	Johnston	Thomas Geoffrey	2018	E1-3
303	*Johnston*	Violet Maud	2003	A8-2
304	Johnston	W.J.	1955	B1-4
305	Johnston	William	1875	A8-2
306	Johnston	William	1947	B1-2
307	Johnston	William	1944	D1-2
308	Johnston	William	1931	TM-A5-2
309	Johnston	William (Sonny)	2011	D3-12
310	Johnston	William Edward	1937	TM-B1-5
311	Johnston	William James	1989	C5-10
312	Johnston	William James	2020	C6-7
313	Johnston	William John	1893	A8-2
314	Johnston	William John	1978	C6-7
315	Johnston	William John	1989	D1-2
316	Johnston	William John (Jack)	1998	D4-2
317	Johnston	William Robert	1967	TM-B1-5
318	Johnston		1937	B5-3
319	Jones	Albert John	1986	C5-7
320	*Jones*	Olive	2021	C5-7
321	Kerr	John		A8-3

Index of Names and Locations

	A	B	C	D
1	**Surname**	**Names**	**Death**	**Location**
322	Kerr	Joseph	1892	A8-3
323	Kerr	Margaret	1896	A8-3
324	Kerr	William John	1896	A8-3
325	Keys	Annabel	1996	A11-2
326	Keys	Anne	1874	A11-3
327	Keys	Charles	1938	A11-2
328	Keys	Charles Jr.		A11-3
329	Keys	Charles Sr.	1879	A11-3
330	Keys	Cheryl		M1
331	Keys	Eliza	1909	C6-2
332	Keys	Eliza Jane	1924	A10-3
333	Keys	Elizabeth	1957	A10-3
334	Keys	Elizabeth		M1
335	Keys	George Victor	2001	A9-1
336	Keys	Irvine	1898	A10-3
337	Keys	Irvine	1902	C6-2
338	Keys	Isabella	1938	A11-2
339	Keys	Jane	1903	A10-3
340	Keys	Lizzie		C6-2
341	Keys	Lizzie Jane	1947	A10-3
342	Keys	Margaret Isobel	1998	A9-1
343	Keys	Mary Eveline	1984	B5-1
344	Keys	Minnie		A10-3
345	Keys	Rebecca Florence	2003	A10-2
346	Keys	Robert Ernest	1979	B5-1
347	Keys	Robert John	1959	A10-3
348	Keys	Samuel	1926	A10-3
349	Keys	Samuel		M1
350	Keys	Samuel (Sam)	2013	A10-2
351	Keys	Samuel Jr.	1974	A10-3
352	Keys	William John	1967	A11-2
353	Kilfedder	Albert John	2016	E1-2

Index of Names and Locations

	A	B	C	D
1	Surname	Names	Death	Location
354	Kilfedder	Annie	1951	B3-4
355	Kilfedder	Catherine	1968	B7-7
356	Kilfedder	Edward J.	1977	B3-4
357	Kilfedder	Elizabeth	1987	B1-10
358	Kilfedder	Florrie	2005	B3-4
359	Kilfedder	James	1942	B7-7
360	Kilfedder	John	1946	B3-4
361	Kilfedder	Robert	1991	B1-10
362	Kilfedder	Samuel	1974	B3-4
363	Kilfedder	Sylvia	2022	E2-5
364	Knox	Alfred	1981	C4-1
365	Knox	Francis	1932	TM-A2-3
366	Knox	John	1935	B6-11
367	Knox	Margaret	1944	B6-11
368	Knox	Margaret	1965	C4-1
369	Knox	Martha Emily	1987	B6-11
370	Knox	Mary Annie	1943	TM-A2-3
371	Knox	William	1955	B6-11
372	Lafferty	Annabella (Cissie)	2007	B6-14
373	Lafferty	Florence	1961	B6-14
374	Lafferty	Kenneth	1964	B6-14
375	Lafferty	Patrick Joseph	1989	B6-14
376	Lafferty	William James	2017	B6-14
377	Leonard	Mary Ann	1942	B4-11
378	Little	Amanda	1978	B6-12
379	Little	Edward	1941	B6-12
380	Little	Elizabeth Mary	1983	B6-12
381	Little	Henry (Harry)	1958	A5-3
382	Little	Henry (Harry) Jr.	1985	A5-3
383	Little	Ivan James	2020	B6-12
384	Little	Robert	1971	B6-12
385	Little	Sarah	1985	A5-3

Index of Names and Locations

	A	B	C	D
1	**Surname**	**Names**	**Death**	**Location**
386	Livingstone	Norman David	1983	B1-9
387	*Livingstone*	Violet Margaret	1971	B1-9
388	*Mack*	Sidney	2014	D4-4
389	*Magovern*	Isabel	1920*	B3-1
390	*Marshall*	Erwin	1904	B4-9
391	Marshall	Eva		B4-9
392	Marshall	Frank H.	1982	TM-A3-2
393	Marshall	George	1917	B4-9
394	Marshall	Hugh	1914	C4-3
395	Marshall	John	1902	B4-9
396	Marshall	Thomas	1903	B4-9
397	*Marshall*	Violet	1993	TM-A3-2
398	*Martin*	Arvina Annabella (Ivy)	2016	D2-12
399	Martin	John James	2019	D2-12
400	McBryde	Ethel Elizabeth	1987	A15-1
401	*McCaskie*	Kathleen		D2-8
402	McClaughry			TM-A1-2
403	McCrea	George Ivan	1996	B7-3
404	McCrea	Rodney Thomas John	2015	B7-3
405	*Millen*	Lily	2009	D4-4
406	*Milligan*	Catherine	1924	C1-4
407	Milligan	Catherine Jane		C1-4
408	Milligan	David		M-2
409	*Milligan*	Ellie	1980	C2-1
410	Milligan	Geo.	1929	C1-4
411	Milligan	John James (Jim)	2004	C2-1
412	Milligan	Joseph		C1-4
413	*Milligan*	Mabel Evelyn	2012	C2-1
414	*Milligan*	Sandra		M-2
415	*Milligan*	Sharron Anne Jayne	2001	B7-2
416	Milligan	Thomas Andrew	2009	C1-1
417	Milligan	Thomas Andrew	1966	C2-1

	A	B	C	D
1	**Surname**	**Names**	**Death**	**Location**
418	Milligan	Trevor Thomas James	2001	B7-2
419	Milligan			A3-1
420	Moffitt	Annie	1968	TM-B1-1
421	Moffitt	Edward	1933	TM-B1-3
422	Moffitt	Elizabeth	1901	TM-B1-1
423	Moffitt	Ellen	1952	TM-B1-3
424	Moffitt	George	1933	TM-B1-1
425	Moffitt	Martha Isabel	2010	TM-B2-2
426	Moffitt	Mary Jane	2017	TM-B1-1
427	Moffitt	Robert	1961	TM-B1-1
428	Moffitt	Susan	1952	TM-B1-1
429	Moffitt	Thomas	1954	TM-B1-1
430	Moffitt	Thomas Andrew	2003	TM-B1-1
431	Moffitt	William George	2016	TM-B2-2
432	Monaghan	David Claude	1999	TM-A8-2
433	Monaghan	Isabella	2013	TM-A8-5
434	Monaghan	Jenny	1985	TM-A8-5
435	Monaghan	Lily	2016	TM-A8-3
436	Monaghan	Thomas	1984	TM-A8-5
437	Montgomery	Caldwell George	1992	C5-1
438	Montgomery	George	1969	C5-1
439	Montgomery	Mary	1969	C5-1
440	Moore	Blanche Elizabeth	1988	C3-1
441	Moore	Florence Kathleen	2017	A13-1
442	Moore	Thomas	1965	C3-1
443	Muldoon			TM-B2-6
444	Murray	John		B4-2
445	Nelson	Alfred	1982	A17-1
446	Nelson	Annabella	1975	A17-1
447	Noble	Gladys	1971	C2-5
448	Noble	John Jr.		B3-1
449	Noble	John Sr.	1878	B3-1

Index of Names and Locations

	A	B	C	D
1	Surname	Names	Death	Location
450	Oldman	George	1985	A14-2
451	*Oldman*	Mary	2003	A14-2
452	Oldman	Thomas James	1987	A14-2
453	Oldman	William George	2016	A14-2
454	Ovens	Joseph	1946	B6-13
455	*Patterson*	Agnes	2000	C7-8
456	Patterson	Arthur	1977	C7-7
457	Patterson	Charles	1979	C7-8
458	Patterson	Ivan	2018	C7-8
459	Patterson	Noel	1978	C7-8
460	Patton	Arthur	1945	A14-2
461	*Patton*	Eleanor	1920	A2-1
462	Patton	John	1900	A2-1
463	*Patton*	Margaret	1958	A14-2
464	Patton	Mary Anne	1902	A2-1
465	Patton	Robert	1900	A2-1
466	*Rankin*	Annabella	1975	B3-8
467	Rankin	David Ryan	1981	B3-8
468	Rankin	John	1968	B3-8
469	Rankin	William	1988	B3-8
470	Reeves	Clive Desmond	2006	B2-4
471	Reeves	Jim		B2-4
472	*Reeves*	Patricia Elizabeth	2003	B2-4
473	*Reeves*	Sarah Ann	1937	B2-4
474	Robinson	Hugh	1973	A14-1
475	Robinson	James	1999	A14-1
476	*Robinson*	Mary	1932	A14-1
477	Scanlon	Alistair Samuel	1998	D4-1
478	*Scanlon*	Elizabeth Margaret	2013	D4-1
479	Scanlon	James Joseph	2001	D4-1
480	Scott	Alexander	1965	B7-4
481	Scott	Mary Ann (Minnie)	1973	B4-15

Index of Names and Locations

	A	B	C	D
1	**Surname**	**Names**	**Death**	**Location**
482	Simpson	Frederick John (Freddie)	2012	TM-B5-2
483	Simpson	James	1977	TM-B2-3
484	Simpson	Mary Anne	1910	B4-3
485	Simpson	Robert	1888	B4-3
486	Simpson	Sadie	1971	TM-B2-3
487	Simpson	Victor James	2015	TM-B2-3
488	Simpson	William George	1923	B4-3
489	Smith	James	1965	B2-10
490	Smith	James		B4-11
491	Smith	Mary Ann	1975	B4-11
492	Speer			A17-2
493	Speer			C2-5
494	Thompson	Freddie	2016	TM-B5-3
495	Thompson	Sadie	2003	TM-B5-3
496	Thompson	William John (Jack)	2020	E2-2
497	Todd	Mary Lena	2009	B7-4
498	Tubman	Betty		B2-4
499	Vance	John		A9-3
500	Vance	Mary	1892	A9-3
501	Vance	Mary Anne	1893	A9-3
502	Vance	Thomas Joseph	2004	D4-7
503	Virtue	David	2004	D4-8
504	Virtue	Elizabeth	1947	B1-6
505	Virtue	Elizabeth	1957	B1-6
506	Virtue	George	1948	B1-6
507	Virtue	Isobella	1958	B1-6
508	Virtue	Jack	1960	D1-8
509	Virtue	James	1937	D1-8
510	Virtue	John	1934	D1-8
511	Virtue	John Wesley	2016	D2-10
512	Virtue	Johnston	1950	B1-6
513	Virtue	Joseph	1975	B1-6

Index of Names and Locations

	A	B	C	D
1	Surname	Names	Death	Location
514	*Virtue*	Margaret Ann	1949	B1-6
515	*Virtue*	Mary Ann	1929	B1-6
516	Virtue	Mary Jane	1928	D1-8
517	Virtue	Noel	1942	B1-6
518	Virtue	Robert George (Bobby)	2000	D1-11
519	*Virtue*	Roseleen	1995	C7-5
520	Virtue	Thomas	1951	B1-6
521	Virtue	Violet Susan	1911	B1-6
522	Virtue	William	1964	C7-5
523	Virtue	William	1947	D1-8
524	Walker	Andrew James	1984	TM-A4-2
525	*Walker*	Anne Jane	1928	TM-A4-3
526	Walker	Cyril		TM-A4-2
527	Walker	David Godfrey	2002	D4-3
528	Walker	Harold		TM-A4-2
529	Walker	Irvine Johnston	1994	D3-4
530	Walker	Kathleen		C5-6
531	*Walker*	Lily	1987	C5-6
532	Walker	Margaret		C5-6
533	*Walker*	Margaret Jane	1996	TM-A4-2
534	*Walker*	Mary Jane	1983	D1-8
535	Walker	Mary Valerie	2018	D3-4
536	Walker	Robert John	1968	D1-8
537	Walker	Tillie J.		TM-A4-3
538	Walker	William James (Jim)	2005	C5-6
539	Walker	William James (Jim)	2009	D1-8
540	Weir	Alexander Dalton	1977	TM-A2-2
541	Weir	Andrew	1945	B7-11
542	*Weir*	Annie	1947	A7-4
543	Weir	David Alfred	1995	B1-1
544	*Weir*	Edith Mary	1993	B3-2
545	*Weir*	Ellen	1962	B4-1

105

Index of Names and Locations

	A	B	C	D
1	**Surname**	**Names**	**Death**	**Location**
546	Weir	George	1978	C4-6
547	Weir	Gretta	1988	C7-9
548	Weir	Helen Elizabeth A.	1993	C4-6
549	Weir	Isabella Anne	1876	B4-2
550	Weir	James	1972	B1-1
551	Weir	James Samuel	1947	TM-A2-2
552	Weir	John	1920	A7-4
553	Weir	John	1962	B4-1
554	Weir	John	1999	C4-6
555	Weir	Margaret Ann	1979	C4-6
556	Weir	Margaret Jane	1973	A7-4
557	Weir	Martha Isobel Jean	2004	B1-1
558	Weir	Martha Jane	1951	B7-11
559	Weir	Mary Ellen	1930	TM-A2-2
560	Weir	Mary Jane	1968	B1-1
561	Weir	Nelson	1992	B3-2
562	Weir	Noel	1995	B1-1
563	Weir	Rev. E.M.		B4-2
564	Weir	Robert (George)	2019	C4-6
565	Weir	Rose	1952	A7-4
566	Weir	Sadie	2005	TM-A2-2
567	Weir	Selina Mary	1965	B3-2
568	Weir	Thomas John	1947	B3-2
569	Weir	William	1985	A7-4
570	Weir	William Herbert	1983	B3-2
571	Weir	William John	1944	B7-11
572	Weir			B4-7
573	Whitcombe	Eileen Mary	1976	A11-1
574	Whitcombe	Laurence	1970	A11-1
575	Wilkin			B4-5
576	Wilson	Arthur Mervyn	1940	C4-4
577	Wilson	Betty	1998	C5-10

Index of Names and Locations

	A	B	C	D
1	Surname	Names	Death	Location
578	Wilson	David	1982	B7-9
579	Wilson	Edward	1892	B6-6
580	Wilson	Elizabeth Mary	1993	B7-9
581	Wilson	Emily	2013	C4-7
582	Wilson	Francis	1949	C4-4
583	Wilson	Francis (Frank)	1992	C4-7
584	Wilson	Francis George	2005	C4-7
585	Wilson	Henrietta	1978	A5-1
586	Wilson	Isabella		B6-6
587	Wilson	James (Jim)	1976	C4-4
588	Wilson	John	1941	A5-1
589	Wilson	Margaret (Peggy)	2009	C4-4
590	Wilson	Margaret Ann	1983	A15-2
591	Wilson	Mary	1944	A5-1
592	Wilson	Mary	1916	C4-4
593	Wilson	Mary	1950	C4-4
594	Wilson	Olie	1981	A15-2
595	Wilson	Robert	1941	A5-1
596	Wilson	Robert	1973	A5-1
597	Wilson	Robert	2020	C5-10
598	Wilson	Sarah	1897	B6-6
599	Wilson	William	1958	C4-4
600	Woods	Annie	1979	B3-3
601	Woods	Anthony	1924	B6-10
602	Woods	Elizabeth Mary	1912	C4-3
603	Woods	Francis	1917	C4-5
604	Woods	Henry	1989	C6-6
605	Woods	Henry George	1916	C4-5
606	Woods	Isabella Jane	2022	B3-3
607	Woods	Jane	1914	C4-3
608	Woods	Joseph	1974	B5-4
609	Woods	Kenneth Russell	1984	B3-3

Index of Names and Locations

	A	B	C	D
1	**Surname**	**Names**	**Death**	**Location**
610	*Woods*	Margaret	1957	C6-6
611	Woods	Margaret Jane	1916	C4-5
612	Woods	Thomas	1957	B3-3
613	Woods	Thomas	2001	B3-3
614	Woods	Thomas Anthony	2012	D3-13
615	Woods	William	1958	C6-6
616	Woods	William Ernest	2019	E2-1

Old and New Irish Genealogy Series Titles

County Antrim

Racavan Burying Ground, Racavan Parish; 895 names. ISBN 978-1-927357-66-8. 2020

County Donegal

Finner Cemetery, Bundoran, Inishmacsaint Parish; 1008 names from Donegal and Leitrim. ISBN 978-1-927357-34-7. 2012

St. Anne's Church of Ireland Cemetery, Ballyshannon, Kilbarron Parish; 1217 names. ISBN 978-1-927357-52-1. 2016

County Fermanagh

Aghalurcher Parish

Holy Cross Roman Catholic Cemetery, Lisnaskea; 1240 names. ISBN 978-1-927357-64-4. 2019

Holy Trinity Church of Ireland Cemetery, Lisnaskea; 1296 names. ISBN 978-1-927357-63-7. 2019

Irish Genealogy Series

Maguiresbridge Church of Ireland Cemetery; 516 names. ISBN 978-1-927357-40-8. 2014

Maguiresbridge Methodist Cemetery; 343 names. ISBN 978-1-927357-41-5. 2014

Maguiresbridge Presbyterian Cemetery; 206 names. ISBN 978-1-927357-42-2. 2014

St. Mary's Roman Catholic Cemetery, Maguiresbridge; 1296 names. ISBN 978-1-927357-68-2. 2020

Aghavea Parish

A Comprehensive Index of the Aghavea Church of Ireland Parish Registers, 1815-1912; over 8300 entries from Aghavea and Aghalurcher parishes. ISBN 978-1-927357-61-3. 2018

Aghavea Church of Ireland Cemetery; 1118 names. ISBN 978-1-927357-38-5. 2013

St. Mary's Roman Catholic Churchyard and Carrickyheenan Road Cemetery, Brookeborough; 692 names. ISBN 978-1-927357-65-1. 2019

Irish Genealogy Series

Boho Parish

Boho Church of Ireland Parish Register; 572 entries ISBN 978-0-9781764-2-6. 2006

Boho Church of Ireland Cemetery; 245 names from Fermanagh and Cavan. ISBN 978-0-9781764-6-4. 2008

St. Faber's Roman Catholic Cemetery; 757 names. ISBN 978-1-927357-01-09. 2011

Cleenish Parish

A Comprehensive Index of the Bellanaleck Church of Ireland Parish Registers (1845-1912); over 742 entries from Fermanagh and Cavan. (CD-ROM) ISBN 978-1-927357-49-1. 2015

Bellanaleck Church of Ireland Cemetery; 624 names. ISBN 978-0-9812063-7-0. 2011

Lisbellaw Church of Ireland Churchyard; 431 names. ISBN 978-1-927357-10-1. 2012

Lisbellaw Presbyterian Cemetery; 110 names. ISBN 978-1-927357-39-2. 2013

Mullaghdun Church of Ireland Cemetery; 354 names. ISBN 978-0-9812063-6-3. 2011

Irish Genealogy Series

A Comprehensive Index of the Mullaghdun Church of Ireland Cleenish Parish Registers (1819-1912); over 2770 entries from Fermanagh and Cavan. ISBN 978-1-927357-35-4. 2013

St. Joseph's Roman Catholic Cemetery, Mullaghdun; 414 names. ISBN 978-1-927357-13-2. 2012

St. Patrick's Holy Well Cemetery, Belcoo; 784 names. ISBN 978-1-927357-58-3. 2017

Templerushin (Holy Well) Graveyard, Belcoo; 82 names ISBN 978-1-927357-57-6. 2017

St. Mary's Catholic Cemetery, Arney; 688 names. ISBN 978-1-927357-78-1. 2025

Derrybrusk Parish

St. Michael's Church of Ireland Cemetery; 393 names. ISBN 978-1-927357-59-0. 2018

Devenish Parish

A Comprehensive Index of the Devenish Church of Ireland Parish Registers; over 6300 entries. ISBN 978-0-9812063-9-4. 2011

Irish Genealogy Series

St. Patrick's Roman Catholic Cemetery, Derrygonnelly; 713 names. ISBN 978-0-9812063-2-5. 2010

Garrison Church of Ireland Cemetery; 304 names from Fermanagh, Leitrim, and Donegal. ISBN 978-0-9781764-7-1. 2008

St. Molaise Church of Ireland Cemetery, Monea; 905 names. ISBN 978-1-927357-00-2. 2012

Monea Roman Catholic Cemetery; 315 names. ISBN 978-0-9869627-4-5. 2011

Drumkeeran Parish

Colaghty Church of Ireland and Tirwinny Methodist Cemeteries; 615 names. ISBN 978-1-927357-75-0. 2025

Tubrid Church of Ireland Graveyard; updated. 575 names. ISBN 978-1-927357-77-4. 2025

Enniskillen Parish

Enniskillen Poor Law Union, Outdoor Relief Register Index: 1847-1899; about 3000 entries from Fermanagh, Tyrone and Cavan. ISBN 978-0-9781764-1-9. 2009

Irish Genealogy Series

Memorials in the Enniskillen Presbyterian Church; 110 names. ISBN 978-1-927357-67-5. 2020

Mount Lourdes Convent Cemetery, Enniskillen; over 2000 names. ISBN 978-1-927357-56-9. 2017

Inishmacsaint Parish

A Comprehensive Index to the Inishmacsaint Church of Ireland Parish Registers, Counties Fermanagh and Donegal (1800-1912); contains over 12,000 entries for Fermanagh, Donegal and Leitrim. ISBN 978-1-927357-55-2. 2016

Benmore Church of Ireland Cemetery; 613 names. ISBN 978-0-9781764-4-0. 2012

Old Derrygonnelly Churchyard; 332 names. ISBN 978-0-9781764-8-8. 2009

Garrison Roman Catholic Cemetery; 1050 names. ISBN 978-0-9812063-0-1. 2009

Slavin Church of Ireland Cemetery; 209 names from Fermanagh and Donegal. ISBN 978-1-927357-19-4. 2012

Three Old Inishmacsaint Parish Graveyards: Inishmacsaint Island, Carrick and Old Slavin; 129 names. ISBN 978-0-9869627-1-4. 2011

Irish Genealogy Series

St. John the Baptist Roman Catholic Cemetery; 595 names. ISBN 978-1-927357-07-01. 2012

Magheracross Parish

Sydare Methodist Cemetery; 1247 names from Fermanagh, Tyrone and Donegal. ISBN 978-0-9781764-9-5. 2008

Two Magheracross Parish Burial Grounds: Old Magheracross Graveyard and the Ballina-mallard Church of Ireland Churchyard; 588 names from Fermanagh and Tyrone. ISBN 978-0-9812063-4-9. 2010

Magheraculmoney Parish

A Comprehensive Index of the St. Mary's Ardess Church of Ireland, Magheraculmoney Parish Registers, County Fermanagh, 1763-1918; 15,630 entries for Fermanagh and Tyrone. ISBN 978-1-927357-71-2. 2021

Edenclaw Catholic Cemetery, Ederney; 579 names. ISBN 978-1-927357-76-7. 2025

Irish Genealogy Series

Rossorry Parish

Rossorry Parish Cemeteries; 1250 names. ISBN 978-0-9781764-0-2. 2009

Trory Parish

Killadeas Church of Ireland Cemetery; 283 names. ISBN 978-1-927357-04-0. 2012

St. Michael's Church of Ireland Cemetery; 320 names. ISBN 978-0-9812063-1-8. 2009

County Leitrim

Kiltyclogher Church of Ireland Churchyard, Cloonclare Parish; 20 names from Leitrim and Fermanagh. ISBN 978-1-927357-70-5. 2020

Old Rossinver Graveyard, Rossinver Parish; 1073 names from Leitrim and Fermanagh. ISBN 978-1-927357-50-7. 2016

Irish Genealogy Series

County Tyrone

St. John's Church of Ireland Churchyard, Fivemiletown, Clogher Parish; 1379 names from Tyrone and Fermanagh. ISBN 978-1-927357-16-3. 2012

St. Joseph's Catholic Cemetery, Fivemiletown, Clogher Parish; 432 names. (in production).

County Wicklow

Old Kilmurry Roman Catholic Cemetery, Newcastle Parish; 187 names. ISBN 978-1-927357-37-8. 2013

For information on where you can obtain any of the preceding titles contact KinFolk Finders by email or phone.

Email: kinfolkfinders154@gmail.com

Phone: 1-519-294-0728.

www.ingramcontent.com/pod-product-compliance
Lightning Source LLC
Chambersburg PA
CBHW061248230426
43663CB00021B/2942